DAVID E FILES II

Preparation Day

Contents

Acknowledgments

First, I would like to give all glory and honor to God because this would not have been possible without Him. I want to thank my mom, dad, and family, who have stood by me through it all and believed in me. Thank you for your prayers, your faith, and your support. I'm truly blessed to have such an awesome family. Thank you for all of the times you stood in prayer for me, and thanks to everyone at Dillworth Church for your prayers and support. We've been through a lot, and I love each of you with all my heart. With God, everything is possible.

Thank you, Laquana, for your support and assistance in making this book possible. Thank you for believing in me when times were challenging and praying for me when doubt and frustration arose. I appreciate you and I love you. May God bless you in mighty ways.

I would like to give a special acknowledgment to all the churches involved in the prison ministry. Your support and faithfulness are much appreciated. The Church of the Highlands is in almost every state prison. I would personally like to thank all of you at the Church of the Highlands for your prayers and support. The volunteers who visit the facilities are amazing people with a heart for God. In every broadcast service, the Church of the Highlands acknowledges the incarcerated inmates as members of the church family. That is much appreciated and means a lot to all of us. The small groups they facilitate provide invaluable assistance to men in ways that are beyond words. Your efforts and generosity are helping change men's lives and enabling light to shine out of darkness. At Bibb County Prison, a Church of the Highlands service baptized me, and the Freedom Conference I attended profoundly transformed my life. You are Jesus' hands and feet, and we love and thank you on behalf of all prisoners!

To all my brothers in Christ at Childersburg Work Release and every other facility: I love you all, and my time there was amazing. The leadership that I witnessed from Pastor Ptomey and Pastor Charles is outstanding. Brothers Jeremy, Detroit, Cash, Prophet, Shaq, and everyone else, may the blessings of the Almighty God be upon you all. In the name of Jesus, I sincerely pray for God's blessings upon everyone who reads this book. May the blessings of God go before you and be in you. May His favor be upon you, and may the Spirit of the Most High God fill you in every way. I pray that the Holy Spirit speaks to you and guides you. I pray that your faith is strengthened and that the Lord Jesus shines on you. We look to You, Lord; our eyes are upon You. In Jesus' name. Amen.

Prologue

The air was thick with anticipation, a silent hum that resonated deep within the hearts of those who dared to listen. For generations, whispers of the Lord's return had ebbed and flowed like tides, sparking both fervor and indifference. Prophets had spoken, scriptures had warned, and yet, the world carried on—burdened with distractions, consumed by its own chaos. But this day was different. A subtle shift had begun, almost imperceptible at first, like the faint stirring of leaves before a storm. Across the earth, signs unfolded, their meanings unmistakable to those with eyes to see and hearts attuned to divine truth. Wars raged and peace faltered, the cries of the oppressed grew louder, and the very ground trembled under the weight of mankind's choices. Nature itself seemed to groan, a celestial call for order in the face of spiraling chaos.

In a quiet corner of the world, a solitary figure knelt in prayer. The room was dimly lit, the only sound the soft whisper of breath and the rustle of pages from a well-worn book. This was no ordinary supplication; it was a plea, a vow, an urgent cry for readiness. For the day was coming—*the* day, foretold by prophets and inscribed in holy writ. The Lord would return, not in secret but with power and great glory, a moment that would split time itself. But were they ready? The question echoed in the hearts of the faithful, tugging at their souls. Preparation was not merely a checklist of deeds or a hollow recital of prayers. It was a transformation—a stripping away of pride, sin, and distractions to reveal hearts fully surrendered. The world called it foolishness, but the faithful called it life.

Time was short. The signs were clearer than ever, like the morning star heralding the dawn. This was the hour to awaken, to shake off the slumber of complacency, and to heed the call. *Prepare the way of the Lord.* As the figure rose from their knees, their hearts were ablaze with resolve. They knew this was more than their journey—it was a mission. A call to the lost, the weary, and the doubtful. A call to light their lamps, to trim the wicks, and to stand ready. Soon, the trumpet would sound, and the skies would split open. The King was coming. And preparation was no longer a suggestion—it was a command.

John 17:6-26 says, *"I have manifested thy name unto the men which thou gavest me out of the world: thine they were, and thou gavest them me; and they have kept thy word. Now they have known that all things whatsoever thou hast given me are of thee. For I have given unto them the words which thou gavest me; and they have received them and have known surely that I came out from thee, and they have believed that thou didst send me. I pray for them: I pray not for the world, but for them which thou hast given me; for they are thine. And all mine are thine, and thine are mine; and I am glorified in them. And now I am no more in the world, but these are in the world, and I come to thee. Holy Father, keep through thine own name those whom thou hast given me, that they may be one, as we are. While I was with them in the world, I kept them in thy name: those that thou gavest me I have kept, and none of them is lost, but the son of perdition; that the scripture might be fulfilled. And now come I to thee; and these things I speak in the world, that they might have my joy fulfilled in themselves. I have given them thy word; and the world hath hated them, because they are not of the world, even as I am not of the world. I pray not that thou shouldest take them out of the world, but that thou shouldest keep them from the evil. They are not of the world, even as I am not of the world. Sanctify them through thy truth: thy word is truth. As thou hast sent me into the world, even so have I also sent them into the world. And for their sakes I sanctify myself, that they also might be sanctified through the truth. Neither pray I for these alone, but for them also which shall believe on me through their word; That they all may be one; as thou, Father, art in me, and I in thee, that they also may be one in us: that the world may believe that thou hast sent me. And the glory which thou gavest me I have given them; that they may be one, even as we are one: I in them, and thou in me, that they may be made perfect in one; and that the world may know that thou hast sent me, and hast loved them, as thou hast loved me. Father, I will that they also, whom thou hast given me, be with me where I am; that they may behold my glory, which thou hast given me: for thou lovedst me before the foundation of the world. O righteous Father, the world hath not known thee: but I have known thee, and these have known that thou hast sent me. And I have declared unto them thy name, and will declare it: that the love wherewith thou hast loved me may be in them, and I in them."*

1

The Power Of The Spoken Word

Luke 23: 50 - 54 says, *"And, behold, there was a man named Joseph, a counsellor; and he was a good man, and a just: (The same had not consented to the counsel and deed of them;) he was of Arimathaea, a city of the Jews: who also himself waited for the kingdom of God. This man went unto Pilate, and begged the body of Jesus. And he took it down, and wrapped it in linen, and laid it in a sepulchre that was hewn in stone, wherein never man before was laid. And that day was the preparation, and the sabbath drew on."*

In this passage of scripture, we learn of a man named Joseph of Arimathea, whom the Bible describes as a good and upright man. He himself was anticipating the arrival of God's Kingdom. This passage takes place in the context of Jesus' recent crucifixion and nailing to the cross. This passage of Scripture takes place as Jesus breathed His last breath and gave up His Spirit. The Bible doesn't say much about Joseph of Arimathea, but this passage says a lot about him. While the disciples were doubting, denying, and watching Jesus' crucifixion in utter horror and disbelief, Joseph was using favor and his position to provide for Jesus' body. The Scripture describes Joseph as a man waiting for the Kingdom of God. Often overlooked, his faith stood out in this otherwise horrific scene. A man waiting for the Kingdom of God can walk by faith, not sight.

Although the situation looked horrible, cruel, and without hope, there was a man whose faith foresaw the current circumstances, and instead of allowing the circumstances to formulate his vision, his faith took action, and as we know, Jesus rose from that tomb victorious. However, the picture of a bloodied and beaten Jesus on that cross didn't look like victory; instead, it appeared as defeat. When we read these passages of Scripture, we often overlook the fact that victory manifested itself as defeat. The greatest, most influential, and most transforming victory of all time came in the form of defeat. Throughout this passage, Joseph of Arimathea's mindset is one of faith working. James 2:17 says, *"In the same way, faith by itself, if not accompanied by action, is dead."*

The book of John 19:38 describes Joseph of Arimathea as a secret disciple of Jesus due to his fear of the Jewish leaders. It is evident from Joseph's description that he believed Jesus to be the Messiah, the Anointed One, because he was a disciple of Jesus. Some may interpret the text as describing Joseph's fear and reluctance to openly express his faith in Jesus. However, if Joseph had been open about his faith in Jesus and had lost his privilege as a council member, he would not have been able to use that privilege to obtain Jesus' body and place it in a tomb that had not yet been occupied, thus fulfilling the prophecy about Jesus' burial. It had to happen this way. Reading these passages of Scripture, it is easy to pass judgment on a situation without full insight into what must take place in order to fulfill prophecy. In the same way, it is easy to pass judgment on a situation in our lives without understanding that it has to happen this way in order to fulfill God's purposes in our lives.

Remember, we walk by faith, not by sight. We have the faith that *"all things work together for the good to those who love God and are called according to His purpose"* (Romans 8:28). The mindset of the disciples during this time is one of doubt, confusion, pain, and unbelief. Here, we examine the actions or in-actions of Jesus' twelve disciples during His crucifixion, burial, and resurrection. These disciples walked daily with Jesus and witnessed firsthand numerous miracles that Jesus had done across the region. Not only did the twelve gain knowledge of who Jesus was by first encountering Him, but they walked with Him daily and listened to His teachings. The twelve witnessed miracles such as the water turning to wine, the feeding of five thousand from five loaves and two fish, Jesus walking on water, the winds and waves obeying Him, the blind seeing, the lame walking, and the dead being raised to life. The disciples witnessed these miracles, as did the evil spirits who submitted to Jesus' commands. Jesus foretold of His death, suffering, and the Resurrection.

Jesus foretold of the Spirit that is to come, the Comforter and Counselor. After hearing Jesus' words and witnessing His works, it appears that the disciples' faith will stand on preparation day. However, as they witnessed the brutality of the beatings and the cries for His death, we must consider the emotions of the twelve and their reactions to the unfolding scenes of the crucifixion. The twelve must have felt doubt lurking inside them as Jesus carried His Cross upon that hill, blood dripping from His stripes and the Crown of Thorns pounded into His skull. The crowds chanted, "If you are the Messiah, then save yourself," as they watched Jesus strapped to the cross and nails pounded through His hands and feet.

Come down from the cross and save yourself! They shouted over and over, taunting the Lord Jesus. The twelve disciples who witnessed many miracles and believed in Jesus also witnessed the cruelty of His death, and in doing so, they were filled with doubt, pain, confusion, and unbelief. The women who had prepared spices returned to the tomb where Jesus lay, only to discover His body was missing. Angels then encountered them, informing them that Jesus had risen. After this discovery, we read in Luke 24:9–11, *"And returned from the sepulchre, and told all these things unto the eleven, and to all the rest. It was Mary Magdalene and Joanna, and Mary the mother of James, and other women that were with them, which told these things unto the apostles. And their words seemed to them as idle tales, and they believed them not."*

This is the mindset of the Twelve Disciples. It's natural for us to read these passages and wonder, "How could they doubt?" Without a comprehensive understanding of their experiences and the depth of their emotions, we are unable to fully comprehend. However, when we, as believers, apply these experiences to our own and understand how our doubt and unbelief evolve, we gain insight and better understand how the Twelve Disciples came to this place of doubt. Throughout our walk with Jesus, we have heard His words and witnessed His work in our lives. Like the Twelve Disciples, who thought the outcome of the Messiah was surely a different path, we experience things in our lives that are different from what we expect. We believe that things should have transpired in a certain manner, and we assume that things will continue to unfold in a similar manner. These experiences leave us in emotional turmoil, where, like the twelve, we will doubt the very words Jesus spoke and begin to lose faith in Him. We become like those who believe in a dead Jesus rather than the Risen Jesus.

I had to reach a certain level of lowness before I completely cried out to Jesus with my whole heart. Having grown up in church and knowing Jesus, I frequently raised my hand to repeat the sinner's prayer at the end of the service, when everyone else was bowing their heads. I believed I was sincere, but I didn't significantly alter my life or perspective. However, what my experiences taught me was that when I finally reached that point in my life, I truly cried out to Jesus.

I've met many people who have had similar experiences in their lives, and we understand the peace that comes from accepting Jesus. As we commit to grow in Him and become disciples, we are to learn from the mistakes of the disciples in Scripture. Often, we will gain insight into similar experiences the disciples had in our own walk with Jesus. Throughout the Gospels, Jesus often called out the Twelve Disciples for their lack of faith. After hearing news of Jesus' resurrection, the Twelve didn't believe the report and thought of it as nonsense. Despite Jesus' prophecy of this event, the Twelve questioned the veracity of His words.

Matthew 20:17-19 says, *"And Jesus going up to Jerusalem took the twelve disciples apart in the way, and said unto them, Behold, we go up to Jerusalem; and the Son of man shall be betrayed unto the chief priests and unto the scribes, and they shall condemn him to death, And shall deliver him to the Gentiles to mock, and to scourge, and to crucify him; and the third day he shall rise again."* The disciples questioned the revealed word of God and viewed it as absurd. Do we take God's spoken word in our lives as nonsense and doubt the words He spoke? Matthew 17:20 says, *"And Jesus said unto them, Because of your unbelief: for verily I say unto you, If ye have faith as a grain of mustard seed, ye shall say unto this mountain, Remove hence to yonder place; and it shall remove; and nothing shall be impossible unto you."*

These are the words of a resurrected Jesus regarding the power and authority of our faith, as well as the spoken word of our mouth. Do we believe His words, or do we count them as nonsense? To understand this passage, we must first understand what faith is. Hebrews 11:1-3 says, *"Now faith is the substance of things hoped for, the evidence of things not seen. For by it the elders obtained a good report. Through faith we understand that the worlds were framed by the word of God, so that things which are seen were not made of things which do appear."*

God's spoken word created the universe from the beginning. He spoke, and

His words created what we see today. Faith is the assurance of the unseen and the confidence in our hopes. The spoken word expresses faith. We understand that grace saves us through faith (Ephesians 2:8). Romans 10:9-10 says, *"That if thou shalt confess with thy mouth the Lord Jesus, and shalt believe in thine heart that God hath raised him from the dead, thou shalt be saved. For with the heart, man believeth unto righteousness; and with the mouth, confession is made unto salvation."*

Oh, the power of the spoken word!

Through my walk with Jesus, I discovered that I used to seek life and speak death. How can this be? How can I have faith in mustard seeds but lack the discipline to control my speech? What do I say in times of struggle and doubt when things don't seem to go my way? "It seems like everything is against me," "I just can't do it anymore," "this never works," "I will never get past this," and "every time I turn around, something bad is happening." On and on throughout my life, though I seek life, I speak death, not understanding the power of the spoken word. Matthew 12:36-37 says, *"But I say unto you, That every idle word that men shall speak, they shall give account thereof in the day of judgment. For by thy words thou shalt be justified, and by thy words thou shalt be condemned."* Could it be that the words I utter, driven by doubt, fear, and anger, aren't directing the mountain into the sea, but rather, they're instructing it to multiply and obstruct my path?

The Power of the Spoken Word.

It is not only possible, but it is also Biblical that my words have the power of life and death. Proverbs 18:21 says, *"Death and life are in the power of the tongue: and they that love it shall eat the fruit thereof."* Throughout my life, I have heard this proverb, not really grasping the significance and magnitude of its meaning. It's an example of believing in a dead Jesus rather than a risen Jesus. By faith in the Risen Jesus, I can take Him at His word and believe in my heart that He is who He says He is, and His words are true. Gaining this knowledge of the Word of God completely transforms and renews the way I think. Romans 12:1-2 says, *"I beseech you therefore, brethren, by the mercies of God, that ye present your bodies a living sacrifice, holy, acceptable unto God, which is your reasonable service. And be not conformed to this world: but be ye transformed by the renewing of your mind, that ye may prove what is that good, and acceptable, and perfect, will of God."* We can't stress enough how crucial it is for everyone. We understand the importance of keeping our mouths shut.

Proverbs 18:6-7 says, *"A fool's lips enter into contention, and his mouth calleth for strokes. A fool's mouth is his destruction, and his lips are the snare of his soul."* In the past, I can't count the number of times my ignorance of this principle has led to my own downfall. Despite my vision and desire for life, the words I utter out of fear ensnare me. Without a doubt, we face an adversary whose primary objective is to steal, kill, and destroy us. However, he is cunning and frequently misleads us, leading us to curse our own path and speak our own doom, all because we remain unaware of his schemes. By gaining this knowledge and applying this principle to our lives, we make a stand against the tactics of the enemy. 2 Corinthians 2:11: *"Lest Satan should get an advantage of us: for we are not ignorant of his devices."*

I used to struggle with drug addiction. Throughout my incarceration, I had given up on life and chose to spend my days attempting to numb my pain the best I could. I had knowledge of Jesus, and I always claimed to have faith that He would somehow make a way for me, but I lived according to my flesh. Many years of slavery tormented me, and I believed I was doing what was best for me. I have great parents who have prayed and interceded for me in mighty ways. I have a church family that prays for me even when I am in a mess. At times, when I was at my lowest, I would reach out to my parents, who would represent me at church, and they would share prophecies about my release. Upon hearing this, I would be filled with joy, but a wave of doubt would soon overwhelm me. Rather than accepting the divine word, I would offer every rational explanation for why it wouldn't materialize. Time after time, despite numerous appeals, I would grow hopeful, only to face rejection. It's like I was seeking life and speaking death.

I finally reached a point in my life where my circumstances had become so dire and hopeless that I was tired of living. I was in lockup at the time, and I sat in that cell, constantly tormented in my mind and fearful of everything. I wanted it to end. I cried out to Jesus, telling Him that if my death in prison was His will, then so be it. I knew that He knew all things, and I've put my trust in that fact. Even if my daily decisions were not in line with Christian living, I knew that He knew. I flushed the remaining drugs I had in my cell, and I cried out with my whole heart. I remembered enough of my childhood experiences in church to know who Jesus was, and I cried to Him. I prayed to Him, telling Him that my life was worthless and that I was tired of living this way. I asked Him to change me and help me, and I surrendered it all to Him. Since then, I've had mistakes and relapses, but everything is different now. In every mistake and relapse, I learned the truth, and though I fell many times, I got back up stronger than before.

At times, my stubbornness and refusal to change led circumstances to demand my attention, which ultimately led me to surrender once more. Honestly, I'm thankful for my trials; though they were unpleasant at the time, I learned valuable truths and became equipped to withstand them. Psalms 119:71 says, *"It is good for me that I have been afflicted; that I might learn thy statutes."* Maybe you are in a season of your life where temptations are ensnaring you. There is hope and deliverance for you. Please pray for Spirit-guided guidance and protection this season. There were times when I felt powerless to withstand my relapses.

As I indulged in whatever substance, I would go to bed full of shame and cry out to God. The next day, I would repeat the cycle. I know the feeling of being powerless to endure. In my sincerity to God and continually pleading for help and understanding, He created circumstances that got my attention and put me back on track. I will admit that the circumstances are uncomfortable and will appear to be evil, causing you to let go. God excels in transforming intended evil into beneficial outcomes. The afflictions that cause you to learn God's truth are not comfortable, but they are necessary, and as you look back, you will be thankful for those afflictions. In this season, find solace, find encouragement, and pay attention to what God is teaching you. He equips the called. His ways are higher than our ways, and His thoughts are higher than our thoughts. In this season, pray for discipline to guard your mouth and not speak evil over your life. If you are struggling, speak deliverance and believe your deliverance is at hand. As you put this principle into practice, the power of the spoken word will come alive in you.

2

Speak Truth To Facts

Luke 7:6-10 says, *"Then Jesus went with them. And when he was now not far from the house, the centurion sent friends to him, saying unto him, Lord, trouble not thyself: for I am not worthy that thou shouldest enter under my roof: Wherefore neither thought I myself worthy to come unto thee: but say in a word, and my servant shall be healed. For I also am a man set under authority, having under me soldiers, and I say unto one, Go, and he goeth; and to another, Come, and he cometh; and to my servant, Do this, and he doeth it. When Jesus heard these things, he marvelled at him, and turned him about, and said unto the people that followed him, I say unto you, I have not found so great faith, no, not in Israel. And they that were sent, returning to the house, found the servant whole that had been sick."*

This Scripture demonstrates the delegation of authority. The centurion understood his own earthly authority and, by faith, understood that spiritual authority through the Word sent from Jesus was all that was needed to accomplish what was desired. Jesus describes the centurion as possessing a great faith that is unparalleled in Israel. As we discussed earlier, we know by faith that the things we see are the result of God's command. Faith in Jesus grants us spiritual authority, and His Holy Spirit actively works within us. Despite the centurion's understanding of his earthly authority and the obedience to his commands, Jesus acknowledges his exceptional faith in distinguishing the Word of Jesus in the spiritual realm, where it manifests in a visible way. Remember that by God's command, all things were created that are seen by the unseen Word of God.

Suppose the local police officers in your city attempted to go to a different state and patrol the streets. Any attempt they made to patrol the streets in a different state would be invalid due to their lack of jurisdiction. Their jurisdiction extends to the city in which they work. When they cross the city limits, they are out of their jurisdiction. They are police officers, but they lack the authority to carry out police business outside of their jurisdiction. We find salvation by accepting Jesus, believing in our hearts that He died for our sins and rose again on the third day. By receiving the Holy Spirit, we have obtained jurisdiction and spiritual authority through His name. Ephesians 3:20 says, *"Now to Him who is able to do immeasurably more than all we ask or imagine, according to His power that is at work within us."*

As believers, it is important to learn how to distinguish between fact and truth. The fact of a situation is what is seen, but the truth of God is able to change facts. For example, when the Israelites were held in slavery in Egypt, God called Moses to be a deliverer. God assured Moses that He was with him and to not be afraid. God sent ten plagues upon Egypt, which prompted Pharaoh to let God's people go. Upon the Exodus of the Israelites from Egypt, they came to the banks of the Red Sea. The truth is, they had nowhere else to turn as the Egyptian army pursued them to take them captive again. The truth is, God said, Let my people go. The truth overshadowed the facts on display as God instructed Moses to stretch forth his staff over the Red Sea, and God sent a mighty wind that parted the sea, allowing the Israelites to cross on dry ground.

The truth overrode the facts, and though the facts were that they were in trouble and the situation looked bad, the truth of what God said changed the facts to align with His Word, and a miracle happened. The Israelites were afraid and even complained to Moses that they would rather be slaves in Egypt than die right here. Many believers become ensnared in this slave mindset, preventing them from embracing what God has in store for them. After witnessing God's miraculous power that freed them from slavery in Egypt, all it took was a fearful situation where the facts were against them, causing them to forget the truth of what God said.

Time and time again, all throughout the Scriptures, the truth overrode the facts. The facts revealed that the army of Israel, surrounded and seemingly destined for destruction, had no chance. But God caused confusion among the opposing armies, so they destroyed themselves. The truth of God overrides the facts. What is the truth that God has spoken over us? Do we tell the truth about the facts in our lives? Do you have the faith of a mustard seed that you know what God said and can speak that truth to the facts in your lives? Or do you allow fear and the facts of your situations to create a slave mentality in which you compromise and lean on your own understanding, speaking out of doubt and fear, not realizing you are your own undoing? There are situations that are fearful, and the facts are overwhelmingly against you. Speak the truth of God to those facts, guard your mouth in trying times, and see the Word of God come alive in your life.

Jeremiah 29:11 says, *"For I know the plans I have for you, declares the LORD, plans to prosper you and not to harm you, plans to give you hope and a future."* This verse is a beacon of hope, a promise that God's intentions for us are rooted in His unwavering love and desire for our ultimate good. When God speaks of prospering us, He is not merely referring to material wealth or worldly success. His plan to prosper us is far greater—it encompasses spiritual growth, eternal blessings, and the fulfillment of His divine purpose in our lives. God's plan to prosper us is rooted in His love and His desire for us to live abundant lives—not just in material terms, but in the fullness of His grace and purpose. When we surrender to His will, trust His timing, and walk in obedience, we position ourselves to receive His blessings. No matter where you are in life, take heart: the God who spoke this promise through Jeremiah is the same God who watches over you today. His plans are for your good, to give you hope and a future that exceeds anything you could imagine. Trust Him, for His plans are always better than ours.

2 Peter 1:3–4 says, *"According as his divine power hath given unto us all things that pertain unto life and godliness, through the knowledge of him that hath called us to glory and virtue: Whereby are given unto us exceeding great and precious promises: that by these ye might be partakers of the divine nature, having escaped the corruption that is in the world through lust."* It is vitally important that you know and understand what the truth of God says in His Word concerning you. You must know your identity in Christ and understand that the promise of His Word applies to you. Gaining this knowledge will equip you to speak these truths to the sometimes unbearable facts of your life. According to Jeremiah, God has plans for you. Despite your doubts and fears, try to create facts that support your path. Speak truth to the facts and rely on the promises God made for you before your creation. Jesus says, Speak to the mountain, and it will obey. Do we trust that the God who creates things out of nothing will keep His promises?

Romans 4:16-21 says, *"Therefore it is of faith, that it might be by grace; to the end the promise might be sure to all the seed; not to that only which is of the law, but to that also which is of the faith of Abraham; who is the father of us all (As it is written, I have made thee a father of many nations,) before him whom he believed, even God, who quickeneth the dead, and calleth those things which be not as though they were. Who against hope believed in hope that he might become the father of many nations, according to that which was spoken, So shall thy seed be. And being not weak in faith, he considered not his own body now dead, when he was about an hundred years old, neither yet the deadness of Sarah's womb: He staggered not at the promise of God through unbelief; but was strong in faith, giving glory to God; And being fully persuaded that, what he had promised, he was able also to perform."*

The facts show that Abraham was old and could not have a son. The facts demonstrate that Sarah was elderly and unable to bear children throughout her entire life. The facts were plain and simple: It's not possible. However, the promises and truth of the Word of God changed what was factual and called into being things that were not. So shall your offspring be that it may be by grace that we obtain through the blood of Jesus. Despite Abraham's imperfections and numerous mistakes, God credited his faith in the spoken word as righteousness throughout his life. Sarah convinced Abraham to sleep with her servant Hagar because she doubted that she would be able to bear a child. Abraham slept with Hagar, and she bore a son. However, God did not make this promise.

After this occurred, Abraham had the choice to accept the fulfillment of the promise by having a son with Hagar rather than continuing to fulfill God's Word. The option of compromise was there. Abraham could have refused to try to get Sarah pregnant and accepted less than what he had promised him. Despite having a son with Hagar, Abraham remained unwavering in his pursuit of the promises God had made to him. Through faith, the truth of God's Word transformed the circumstances, leading Sarah to conceive a son in accordance with God's Word.

Your situation may seem hopeless and insurmountable. However, we serve a God of all possible. Speak life into your situation and circumstances. When doubt and fear are flooding your thoughts, guard your mouth not to speak those doubts and fears. Instead, implement the principles of guarding your mouth and speaking life. Deuteronomy 30:19 says, *"I call heaven and earth to record this day against you, that I have set before you life and death, blessing and cursing: therefore choose life, that both thou and thy seed may live."*

I have spent a lot of my life thinking I was choosing life, but the words I am speaking are reflective of death. Whether it's goals I'm seeking to accomplish or a vision that God has shown me of works to do, in my mind doubt arises or fear of failure and rejection. I will play out scenarios in my mind of failing to accomplish things and what happens if this happens or if that happens because of this, and I've created a path for failure. I would even speak those fears to friends and family and attempt to downplay my procrastination by thinking negatively about the work I am to do, not realizing I'm speaking death or curses over my future.

Then, I wonder why things are blocking my progress or why such difficulties are coming my way. Here I am, then, rebuking the devil for causing situations to arise in my path that I spoke over myself without even realizing what I was doing. As I come to this realization of myself before God, my reaction is that of Isaiah 6:5 which says, *"Then said I, Woe is me! for I am undone; because I am a man of unclean lips, and I dwell in the midst of a people of unclean lips: for mine eyes have seen the King, the Lord of hosts."* The process of renewing our mind and the spirit of our mind is about truly trusting in the promises of God and what He said to us. Though the facts in our lives are against us, what did God say? Do I believe what God said, or do I allow my circumstances and the things I can see against me to distract me in such a way that I speak against what God has said? I have had to learn to control my thoughts in this area. It's a process of trial and error.

I make mistakes every day fighting this battle, but I'm committed to mastering my tongue, especially in relation to my life and future. What am I allowing to control my thoughts? What thoughts am I dwelling on and speaking about? What is the process of renewing my mind? In John chapter 2, we read of where Jesus clears the Temple Courts. John 2:13-16 says, *"And the Jews' Passover was at hand, and Jesus went up to Jerusalem. And found in the temple those that sold oxen and sheep and doves, and the changers of money sitting: And when he had made a scourge of small cords, he drove them all out of the temple, and the sheep, and the oxen; and poured out the changers' money, and overthrew the tables; And said unto them that sold doves, Take these things hence; make not my Father's house an house of merchandise."*

To gain an understanding of this passage of Scripture, we must first know that we are the temple of God. 1 Corinthians 3:16 says, *"Know ye not that ye are the temple of God, and that the Spirit of God dwelleth in you?"* By understanding this and reading the account of Jesus clearing the Temple Court, it takes on a different light. The Jewish Temple consisted of two gates. The outer gates and the inner gates. The area between the two gates was known as the Temple Courts. Inside the inner gate was the Holy Place, and inside the Holy Place was the Holy of Holiness. It was inside the outer gate, known as the Temple Courts, where sacrificial items were bought and sold. Deals were made in the temple courts, and money was exchanged. Knowing that we are God's temple, how does this apply to us? The outer gates are representative of our eyes and ears. What are we watching and listening to?

The Temple Courts are our minds, where we are tempted to offer sacrificial items to idols of our temptations. It's in our minds where deals are made that compromise our intentions. I can fornicate in my mind, usually after watching or seeing something that triggers a memory or desire, and I will utilize my imagination, which will drive me to seek out my desire and take action. The buying and selling of cattle and sheep. Inside the temple courts of my mind, I will allow fear and doubt to flood my thoughts of failure and rejection, usually by hearing other people's opinions and their failures. These stories of failure that I listen to and my own past experiences, coupled with factual circumstances in my life, make what God said concerning me seem impossible. So, I will settle for a compromised agreement in my mind and take less than what God has for me. The exchanging of coins at the money tables.

Jesus gives us a clear illustration of the clearing of the Temple Courts that is alive, powerful, and necessary for the renewing of our minds. This is an illustration of what takes place in the spiritual realm as we speak the Word of God over our mind and our lives. We have to utilize and apply the authority given to us by the Holy Spirit. This fight is against spiritual forces that influence the mind and manipulate emotions in people to cause circumstances that stand against us. Our enemy is not flesh and blood. Although the influence of spiritual wickedness is often carried out in willing vessels of flesh and blood, we are not against flesh and blood.

2 Corinthians 10:3-5 says, *"For though we walk in the flesh, we do not war after the flesh. (For the weapons of our warfare are not carnal, but mighty through God to the pulling down of strong holds;) Casting down imaginations, and every high thing that exalteth itself against the knowledge of God, and bringing into captivity every thought to the obedience of Christ."* Knowing that our battle is fought in the spiritual realm, we are given knowledge and power over the thoughts that influence that war in our minds, or temple courts. We must take back control of what we think. When my mind is flooded with thoughts of failure and I begin to imagine the failure and see how it could happen, I use the Word of God to cast down those imaginations and hold those thoughts captive to the obedience of Jesus. When I utilize this Scripture against the war brewing in my mind, it's the image of Jesus with a whip of cords driving out those who are buying and selling in my temple courts.

I CAST DOWN THESE IMAGINATIONS AND HOLD ALL THOUGHTS CAPTIVE TO THE OBEDIENCE OF JESUS. Throughout the day, as you live your life and thoughts flood your mind in an attempt to create imagination, you have the Word of God as your sword in the Spirit Realm. In a world full of corruption and violence, we have weapons that maintain peace, not as the world gives but as Jesus gives. John 14:27 says, *"Peace I leave with you; my peace I give you. I do not give you what the world gives. Do not let your hearts be troubled, and do not be afraid."* Peace, in a worldly sense, is absent from war. Peace, as the world gives, is without war. Jesus describes peace as something He gives, which is not like the world. The peace Jesus gives is in the midst of our war, and the war we fight is not carnal; it is spiritual. Spiritual peace will surpass our understanding. When everything is against us, we can have peace, knowing that He will never leave us or forsake us. Through the storms that life brings, we can have His peace. Speak to the mountains and proclaim His peace in your life.

Ephesians 6:12 says, *"For our struggle is not against flesh and blood, but against the rulers, against the authorities, against the powers of this dark world, and the spiritual forces of evil in the heavenly realms."* As we grow in our knowledge of God's Word and gain an understanding of the war we fight, we become more aware of our own actions. If we are honest with ourselves, we can see the enemy at work in us in certain situations where we have to ask for forgiveness from people we offended. In these times, we are ashamed of how we acted or responded to certain things. Looking back over my life, I see the enemy work where I was manipulated into thinking certain ways that at the time I thought I was right, but I would be wrong. I know how the enemy can play with our emotions, creating thought patterns that attempt to control our minds to see things a certain way, and in doing so, we deprive others of the benefit of doubt and rush to judgment against them. I have had to seek the forgiveness of others countless times due to my own shortcomings. It's in this understanding that I have learned to forgive as well.

The same way the enemy can deceive me and use me in negative ways, he will use others against me. Having knowledge of spiritual warfare enables you to see not the person attacking you but the spiritual force driving them into action using the same deceitful tactics he has used on you before. Having this knowledge will enable you to truly forgive those who have wronged you because you have the understanding to see not the person but the spirit you are at war against. This will give you compassion for the person and aid you in forgiveness. It's not easy, but it gets easier. Thanks be to Jesus for His power and strength.

3

Balaam's Error

In the book of Revelations, Jesus warns the church in Pergamum about some who hold to the teachings of Balaam. Revelation 2:14 says, *"Nevertheless, I have a few things against you: There are some among you who hold to the teachings of Balaam, who taught Balak to entice the Israelites to sin, so that they ate food sacrificed to idols and committed sexual immorality."* In our understanding of the Scripture of Jesus' warning to the Church of Pergamum, it would be wise to study Balaam's error. The Book of Numbers contains the account of Balak summoning Balaam. Balak, King of Moab, is terrified of the Israelites due to their number. As Balak had seen what the Israelites had done to the Amorites, he was frightened by their proximity to his territory and called Balaam to curse them.

Numbers 22:5-6 says, *"He sent messengers therefore unto Balaam the son of Beor to Pethor, which is by the river of the land of the children of his people, to call him, saying, Behold, there is a people come out from Egypt: behold, they cover the face of the earth, and they abide over against me: Come now therefore, I pray thee, curse me this people; for they are too mighty for me: peradventure I shall prevail, that we may smite them, and that I may drive them out of the land: for I wot that he whom thou blessest is blessed, and he whom thou cursest is cursed."* So Balak sent messengers to Balaam along with a fee of divination, and as the elders of Moab and Midian found Balaam, they told him what Balak said in the previous verse. Balaam's response is where we pick up in verses 8–12.

Numbers 22:8-12 says, *"And he said unto them, Lodge here this night, and I will bring you word again, as the Lord shall speak unto me: and the princes of Moab abode with Balaam. And God came unto Balaam, and said, What men are these with thee? And Balaam said unto God, Balak the son of Zippor, king of Moab, hath sent unto me, saying, Behold, there is a people come out of Egypt, which covereth the face of the earth: come now, curse me them; peradventure I shall be able to overcome them, and drive them out. And God said unto Balaam, Thou shalt not go with them; thou shalt not curse the people: for they are blessed."*

Balaam reported this command from God to the messengers, informing them that the Lord refused to let Balaam go with them. As the officials reported this news to Balak, he did what the enemy will do in our lives today. Numbers 22:15 says, *"And Balak sent yet again princes, more, and more honourable than they."* In my life, I have discovered that more numerous and distinguished versions of the same temptation will cause me to question what God really said about the issue. I know that there are things in my life that I struggle with, and I know what God's Word says about them, but a more numerous and distinguished representation of those things can leave me thinking it's not that bad. In these situations, the enemy will attempt to distort God's Word to deceive you into thinking God spoke differently or didn't mean what we thought it meant in the first place. Remember the first tactic used by the serpent in the Garden of Eden?

Genesis 3:1 says, *"Now the serpent was more subtil than any beast of the field which the Lord God had made. And he said unto the woman, Yea, hath God said, Ye shall not eat of every tree of the garden?"* It's no secret that the enemy employs certain tactics to lure you into making mistakes. In the case of Adam and Eve, it was the downfall of all mankind. Here, the enemy is using a prophet to make a profit and curse the chosen people of God. Balaam's first major error is questioning the unchanging Word of God, allowing the enemy to distort his understanding of what God said. The enemy employs more numerous and distinguished forms of manipulation and temptation, preying on the evil desires that lurk in our flesh. In this case, the weakness was greed. Balak's offers were more numerous and distinguished, consisting of a handsome reward and the promise to do what Balaam said.

Numbers 22:18-20 says, *"And Balaam answered and said unto the servants of Balak, If Balak would give me his house full of silver and gold, I cannot go beyond the word of the Lord my God, to do less or more. Now therefore, I pray you, tarry ye also here this night, that I may know what the Lord will say unto me more. And God came unto Balaam at night, and said unto him, If the men come to call thee, rise up, and go with them; but yet the word which I shall say unto thee, that shalt thou do."* After reading this passage, it is easy to conclude that Balaam did what was right. He sought God concerning the issue and followed what God said was right. Remember the first words from the Lord to Balaam in verse 12: *"Thou shalt not go with them; thou shalt not curse the people: for they are blessed."* However, a more numerous and more distinguished version caused Balaam to seek a different response from the Lord because the Prophet could see a profit for himself. Balaam had allowed compromise to enter his heart through the deceptive nature of the enemies of God's people. Balaam knew he could not curse what God had blessed, so he developed a plan. The Scriptures teach us that God does not lie or change His mind.

Numbers 23:19 says, *"God is not a man, that he should lie; neither the son of man, that he should repent: hath he said, and shall he not do it? or hath he spoken, and shall he not make it good?"* Having knowledge of this truth enables you to see the deceptive nature of the enemy behind the scenes, attempting to distort the Word of God as he did in the Garden. By continuing to read these passages, we learn that God was angry at Balaam's decision to go with the officials. Numbers 22:21-22 says, *"Balaam got up in the morning, saddled his donkey, and went with the Moabite officials. However, God was very angry when he went, and the Angel of the Lord stood in the road to oppose him. Balaam was riding on his donkey, and his two servants were with him."*

So the Scriptures say that God was very angry that Balaam went with the Moabite officials. If God had instructed Balaam to go, it wouldn't make sense for God to be so angry and send the Angel of the Lord to oppose him. The enemy deceived Balaam and distorted his initial understanding of God's words. We can learn a valuable lesson from a different form of deception. The serpent in the Garden of Eden used a similar tactic, but this one is more numerous and distinguished. As believers, it is critical that we know the Word of God concerning us. It is evident that the enemy attempts to distort the Word of God in our minds, using our evil desires as bait to manipulate our emotions and create imaginations of evil desire disguised as vision, which is in fact only a daydream of corrupted thinking for selfish gain, and attempts to use the Word of God to affirm it. God has given you a vision of good works that He predestined for you before the foundations of the earth.

Ephesians 2:10 says, *"For we are God's handiwork, created in Christ Jesus to do good works, which God prepared in advance for us to do."* God will reveal to us a work to do. The enemy will attempt to distort that vision and create in you a desire for selfish gain. The enemy comes to steal, kill, and destroy. He uses us through deception and manipulation, preying on evil desires from past experiences and a former way of life that looks appealing and harmless. It is our duty to know what God really says about us. Your true vision will manifest in a work that reaches others and demonstrates God's love. The enemy takes that vision and tries to instill doubt and fear in you, convincing you that it's impossible. Unfortunately, most believers lack the knowledge to guard their mouths and instead speak words of their own undoing based on thoughts of doubt and fear. You must possess the faith of a mustard seed and the discipline to keep your mouth safe.

Balaam was in error, and though the thoughts of his payday drove him to distort what God said, God's mercy was working to change his reckless path. God sent forth the Angel of the Lord to stand in his path. Numbers 22:23-32 says, *"When the donkey saw the Angel of the Lord standing on the road with a drawn sword in his hand, it turned off the road and into a field."* To get it back on the road, Balaam beat it. Then the Angel of the Lord stood in a narrow path through the vineyards, with walls on both sides. When the donkey saw the Angel of the Lord, it pressed close to the wall, crushing Balaam's foot against it. He then beat the donkey again. Then the Angel of the Lord moved ahead and stood in a narrow place with no room to turn right or left. When the donkey saw the Angel of the Lord, it lay down under Balaam, who became angry and beat it with his staff.

Then the Lord opened the donkey's mouth, and it said to Balaam, What have I done to you to make you beat me these three times? Balaam answered the donkey: You have made a fool of me! If only I had a sword in my hand, I would kill you right now. The donkey said to Balaam, Am I not your own donkey, which you have always ridden to this day? Have I gotten used to doing this to you? No, he said. Then the Lord opened Balaam's eyes, and he saw the Angel of the Lord standing in the road with his sword drawn. So he bowed low and fell facedown. The Angel of the Lord asked him, Why have you beaten your donkey these three times? I have come here to oppose you because your path is a reckless one before me.

This Scripture passage is well-known for its humorous depiction of the talking donkey. However, a careful examination of these passages and a deep understanding of spiritual truth reveal God's ways to us, even when we are in error and on a reckless path. The passage starts as the Angel of the Lord stands in the path with His sword drawn, and the donkey leaves the road into a field. I want you to imagine a donkey in your life's circumstances. As you embark on your journey, a disruption occurs in your usual routine. This disruption forces you to make a few adjustments to get things back on track, but they should not be too severe. As you navigate through a challenging period in your life, unexpected events often arise, causing you to feel as though the walls are closing in on you. You suffer through it, and in your mind, you blame the devil for causing such discomfort and inconvenience in your life. You are filled with frustration, and you even find yourself cursing the circumstances as they unfold.

Just as you begin to get things back in order and continue on your path, everything shuts down on you. You look to the left and to the right, and no one is there to help you. You curse your circumstances, and you are so frustrated that you begin to talk to yourself about how everything is wrong. Then, as you finally realize something isn't right, you remember that these things haven't happened this way before. In your desperation, you cry out to Jesus, and clarity begins to pour in, revealing that your path is reckless. You receive confirmation, and you realize you are in error. When these things happen in your life, check your motives for why you are pursuing this path. Take a deep look at yourself and determine what is driving you down this reckless path.

Balaam had this experience and even confessed it, but he was unable to overcome his motives; despite experiencing supernatural and divine intervention, he still desired to continue. The Angel of the Lord permitted him to continue even after revealing himself to Balaam and expressing that his path was reckless. It's easy to look at Balaam's disobedience and error and say, How could he go on after that? It seems like he would have caught on. As I look back on my life, I ask myself these same questions. How did I continue on my reckless path after warnings and clarity? How could I? What was driving me?

I can reflect on a sinful past in which I disregarded warnings and let addiction rule my actions. I wanted to make money, get high, and have fun with friends. Living carelessly and recklessly meant that my destruction was just around the corner. I had no knowledge of spiritual warfare or any other spiritual concepts. Despite growing up in church, I struggled to understand its teachings. Now, as I reflect on the times in my past since truly giving my life to Jesus and embracing His truths, I can relate more to this story of Balaam and the talking donkey.

I often wonder how many times I blamed the devil for inconveniences in my life instead of realizing Jesus was trying to get my attention. Is it possible that I rebuke Jesus in His name because my ignorance led me to believe it was an attack by the enemy? I've realized that the process of sanctification will involve making mistakes and learning from them. Thank you, Jesus, for your grace. The Scriptures teach us about celestial beings and the peril of mistreating them. In the book of Jude, it talks about ungodly people who pervert the grace of our God into a license for immorality and deny Jesus Christ, our only sovereign and Lord. The Book of Jude presents instances of rebellion by individuals saved from slavery in Egypt who later faced destruction due to their lack of faith. It also discusses the angels who abandoned their positions of power, remaining in darkness and ensnared in eternal chains for judgment. It gives the example of Sodom, Gomorrah, and the surrounding towns, which gave themselves up to sexual immorality and perversion.

These serve as an example of those who suffer the punishment of eternal fire. From this point on, Jude speaks in verses 8–11, "*In the exact same way, on the strength of their dreams, these ungodly people pollute their own bodies, reject authority, and heap abuse on celestial beings. However, even the Archangel Michael, in a dispute with the devil regarding Moses' body, refrained from condemning him for slander, instead declaring, "The Lord rebuke you!" They slander what they don't understand, and what they do understand instinctively, like irrational animals, will destroy them. Woe to them! They have followed Cain's path, hurried into Balaam's mistake for financial gain, and perished in Korah's rebellion. "*

Balaam's first mistake was to compromise God's Word by listening to temptation and distorting what God said. Balaam commits another major mistake by disregarding the Angel of the Lord, who stands in his path. Balaam recognized his error, and instead of correcting it based on the efforts of God to get his attention, he sought to continue on. Numbers 22:33-34 says, *"The donkey saw me and turned away from me three times. If it hadn't turned away, I would have certainly killed you by now, but I would have spared it. Balaam said to the Angel of the Lord, I have sinned. I did not realize you were standing in the road to oppose me. Now if you are dissatisfied, I will go back."*

It appears that the Angel of the Lord, standing in my way and cautioning me about my reckless path, would not question His displeasure. Driven by evil desire, my stubbornness and blindness not only lead me to question God's Word, but also to doubt God's workings in my life. Like Balaam, I would resort to beating the donkey, who was only acting under the authority of the Angel of the Lord. How can I, as a believer and one who confesses the Lord Jesus Christ as Lord and Savior, resort to thinking that He is not in control of my life? Jesus stated, "You will face troubles and tribulations in this world, but rest assured, I have conquered it." He is in control. When I come to truly believe and trust in this truth, then I can echo the words of Job: *"Though He slay me, I will trust in Him"* (Job 13:15).

Balaam, after having his eyes opened and confessing his fault, still sought to continue on his reckless path. Although Balak had summoned Balaam to curse the Israelites in order to defeat them, Balaam confessed that he could not curse what God had blessed. However, Balaam conspired in his heart to devise a plan to entice the Israelites by sending women among them to commit sexual immorality. Balaam understood that God would punish such acts among His people. Balaam knew that God's chastening of His people for their acts would appear to the Moabites as a curse, but he could keep his reward from Balak. Balaam could not openly speak a curse on the people of God, but he knew how to trick the people to curse themselves through temptation. Balaam tempted the Israelite men by bringing in women who appealed to their flesh, leading them to succumb to those temptations.

Numbers 25:1-3 says, *"And Israel abode in Shittim, and the people began to commit whoredom with the daughters of Moab. And they called the people unto the sacrifices of their gods: and the people did eat, and bowed down to their gods. And Israel joined himself unto Baalpeor: and the anger of the Lord was kindled against Israel."* Following the actions of the Israelite men, a curse appeared, marking God's judgment to free His people from their yokedness to the Baal of Peor. He sent a plague into the land, which killed 24,000 Israelites. Phinehas, acting with zeal, took his spear and killed the Israelite man who had brought the Moabite woman before Moses and the entire assembly, while they were weeping at the entrance of the tent of meeting. He struck them both dead, and after this, God spoke to Moses.

Numbers 25:10-13 says, *"And the Lord spake unto Moses, saying, Phinehas, the son of Eleazar, the son of Aaron the priest, hath turned my wrath away from the children of Israel, while he was zealous for my sake among them, that I consumed not the children of Israel in my jealousy. Wherefore say, Behold, I give unto him my covenant of peace: And he shall have it, and his seed after him, even the covenant of an everlasting priesthood; because he was zealous for his God, and made an atonement for the children of Israel.*" Balaam caused the death of 24,000 Israelites by teaching Balak to entice them to commit these sins in the sight of God. Balaam allowed greed to control his thoughts and drive him. A valuable lesson from the teachings of Balaam is for us as believers today to not allow greed to control our thoughts so that we become stumbling blocks to other believers. In prison, I used to sell drugs to help make ends meet.

I would attend chapel services, give thanks to God, and pray. I would return to the dorm and serve alcohol to others. I had yet to learn the lessons of ill-gotten gains and how to avoid becoming a hindrance. In my mind, I would listen to the lies of the enemy, trying to justify my behavior, saying that if I didn't sell it to them, someone else would, so it might as well be me who profits. This lie made me believe I was not in the wrong. Before the Lord opened my eyes to see that my path was reckless before Him, I had to navigate through a journey of walls closing in and pain. In my walk with Jesus, I can admit my faults because I know He is with me.

Understanding spiritual truths will teach you that, as a child of God, people may try to curse you, but ultimately only you have the power to curse yourself. This truth is exemplified by Balaam. Balak didn't have the power to curse the Israelites; he summoned Balaam. Balaam didn't have the power to curse the Israelites; he taught Balak how to entice them to curse themselves. However, the appearance of cursing themselves brought purification, which was actually a blessing. Victory comes in the form of defeat. God is capable of taking every shortcoming and using it for your benefit. Can you trust him with the process? Once you understand that, even in the face of defeat, He is working for your good, and you firmly believe in this, you will exercise the faith of a mustard seed, beginning to cast mountains out of your life's path.

4

Peace

2 Corinthians 6:1-2 says, *"We then, as workers together with him, beseech you also that ye receive not the grace of God in vain. (For he saith, I have heard thee in a time accepted, and in the day of salvation have I succoured thee: behold, now is the accepted time; behold, now is the day of salvation.)"* On preparation day, everything Jesus was preparing His disciples for came alive as He Himself died on the cross. Jesus' resurrection fulfilled His promise and gave His word power. The sending of the Holy Spirit brought the power of His Word and made it active and alive in us through the Holy Spirit. His power is now active in us as believers.

Romans 8:10-11 says, *"And if Christ be in you, the body is dead because of sin; but the Spirit is life because of righteousness. But if the Spirit of him that raised up Jesus from the dead dwell in you, he that raised up Christ from the dead shall also quicken your mortal bodies by his Spirit that dwelleth in you."* Understanding our spiritual authority through faith in Jesus and the power operating within us should comfort us, as we know that nothing is impossible. Time after time, throughout my life, I look at the situation and what the facts say. I would observe the situation and attempt to rationalize how God could orchestrate a favorable outcome for me. If God guides this person to act in this way, and I am able to make it happen in this manner, then it will indeed work, praise be to God. When it falls apart, I doubt everything all over again and begin to question God about why this is not happening for me. The Spirit troubled me during these times, and I struggled to discern God's plan for my life.

When this happened many times, I would slip backwards into drinking or getting high again to ease the pain. I would revert to my old habits, like a dog returning to its own vomit. Every time God would pick me back up, I would learn a little more about myself and the faithfulness of a loving God. I came across teachings about the laws of attraction and using the subconscious mind. I prayed to God, asking Him to reveal His truth to me through His Word. He showed me the meaning of faith, the power of the words we speak, and the promises of His Word. I began to study and apply these principles of faith, using discipline to guard my mouth and speak life over every situation. Throughout this process, the Scriptures came alive to me, and I began to grow spiritually through meditation on His Word and seeking His direction.

Situations in my life that used to bring me downcast and distraught, prompting me to speak negatively about them, now serve as opportunities for me to express my faith and speak truth to facts. Does every situation change to my benefit? No, but my soul finds rest, my spirit gains strength, and my confidence rests in Him who creates the path. I only use what He gives me. I gain knowledge from His Word, gain wisdom from my mistakes, and comprehend how to utilize it in my life. Experiencing the peace of God is something I cherish, and knowing He is with me through every storm means I will speak His truth about me in every situation I face.

2 Corinthians 6:3–10 says, *"Giving no offence in any thing, that the ministry be not blamed: But in all things approving ourselves as the ministers of God, in much patience, in afflictions, in necessities, in distresses, In stripes, in imprisonments, in tumults, in labours, in watchings, in fastings; By pureness, by knowledge, by long*

suffering, by kindness, by the Holy Ghost, by love unfeigned, By the word of truth, by the power of God, by the armour of righteousness on the right hand and on the left, By honour and dishonour, by evil report and good report: as deceivers, and yet true; As unknown, and yet well known; as dying, and, behold, we live; as chastened, and not killed; As sorrowful, yet alway rejoicing; as poor, yet making many rich; as having nothing, and yet possessing all things."

In the midst of it all is God's unfailing love. He gives us strength to endure and empowers us, through His Spirit, to speak His words. Having God's peace necessitates having peace with God. We can seek to have artificial peace as the world gives it, but often this peace is very temporary and, in the end, only adds to the misery. It took me years and numerous failures to come to the realization that there is no peace in a bottle. At the time, it seemed like a remedy, but that's the deception taking root. Day after day, you will seek that kind of peace, and it will only grow worse. To have peace with God, you will gain inner peace, which leads to peace with others.

Romans 5:1-2 says, *"Therefore, we have peace with God through our Lord Jesus Christ, through whom we have gained access by faith into this grace in which we now stand, and we boast in the hope of God's glory."* Jesus is the gateway to having peace with God. There is no other way of obtaining peace with God. The enemy knows this truth and will attempt to deceive you into thinking there is another way. These other ways will have a form of godliness, but deny the power thereof. Jesus is powerful. Only through Jesus do we gain access to the Holy Spirit, which is the power of God.

The Hebrew word for peace is *shalom*. People often use it to describe the appearance of calm and tranquility in individuals, groups, and nations. Translations often translate the Greek word *"eirene"* as peace, implying unity and accord. In his writings, Paul frequently uses *eirene* to describe the New

Testament Church's objectives. But the deeper, more foundational meaning of peace is the spiritual harmony brought about by an individual's restoration to God, as spoken of in Romans 5:1-2, *"Therefore being justified by faith, we have peace with God through our Lord Jesus Christ: By whom also we have access by faith into this grace wherein we stand, and rejoice in hope of the glory of God."* Once we have peace with God, we experience God's peace.

Philippians 4:7 says, *"And the peace of God, which transcends all understanding, will guard your hearts and your minds in Christ Jesus."* In Greek, the word for peace mentioned in Philippians 4:7 is *"phroureo."* This word refers to the act of guarding and receiving protection from a military guard, either to thwart a hostile invasion or to prevent the inhabitants of a besieged city from fleeing. *Phroureo* is the feeling of conviction that protects us from taking in images and entertaining thoughts the enemy uses to entice us to sin. Deception is the act of bringing to mind the pleasures of those particular sins without allowing you to think of the negative consequences that result from them. Chapter 2 mentions the cleansing of the temple courts.

Having God's peace is our protection. I frequently hear new believers talk about how things they used to do don't feel the same anymore or aren't as appealing as they once were. This is *Phroureo,* "the peace of God," at work in you, guarding you. Having peace with God and the peace of God in your life gives you spiritual authority through Jesus to set the atmosphere where you are. During my incarceration, I experienced a constant presence of violence around me. Fights would break out, and people on drugs could hear voices, causing paranoia. In these situations, I first realized the power of spiritual authority when I began to proclaim peace while still in the dorm. I would pray in the Spirit, confront any spirit of anger and hate, and declare the restoration of peace in Jesus name. I wouldn't stand in front of the dorm loudly proclaiming this prayer. I would silently pray it on my bed, using the authority I have through Jesus to battle the spirits that cause confusion and violence. The tension in the dorm release was palpable, and the violence would cease.

When I first experienced this, I shared it with a friend in the dorm, to which he responded with a disbelieving look. However, at that moment, no one could refute what I had just witnessed. I knew from this experience how real spiritual warfare truly is, and more importantly, I discovered the spiritual authority I have through Jesus. If you are not careful, a state of contentment can lead to complacency. Complacency does not bring God glory. However, in times of storms and tribulations, you will access the peace of God, which magnifies His presence and brings glory to His name.

Luke 8:22-25 says, *"Now it came to pass on a certain day, that he went into a ship with his disciples: and he said unto them, Let us go over unto the other side of the lake. And they launched forth. But as they sailed he fell asleep: and there came down a storm of wind on the lake; and they were filled with water, and were in jeopardy. And they came to him, and awoke him, saying, Master, master, we perish. Then he arose, and rebuked the wind and the raging of the water: and they ceased, and there was a calm. And he said unto them, Where is your faith? And they being afraid wondered, saying one to another, What manner of man is this! for he commandeth even the winds and water, and they obey him."*

Scripture illustrates Jesus' authority, demonstrating His control over even the laws of nature. Despite His ability to calm the storm, Jesus was more concerned about the disciples' lack of faith during this challenging time. Upon reading this passage, it appears that the Disciples acted in a manner similar to what any of us would have done in their situation. They roused Jesus from His sleep and expressed their fear. I'm grateful for the disciples' lack of faith in these circumstances, as their example teaches me how to apply faith in my own life, knowing that Jesus is in the boat with me. Knowing and understanding that Jesus is with you in the storm gives you the authority to speak truth to the facts as they rage around you. Peace be still!

These are God's words in times of trouble, and these are the words we should speak by faith, knowing who we are in Him. The storm subsided as Jesus spoke. The storms will subside in you as you speak His words to them. Mark 6:45-52 says, "*And straightway he constrained his disciples to get into the ship, and to go to the other side before unto Bethsaida, while he sent away the people. And when he had sent them away, he departed into a mountain to pray. And when even was come, the ship was in the midst of the sea, and he alone on the land. And he saw them toiling in rowing; for the wind was contrary unto them: and about the fourth watch of the night he cometh unto them, walking upon the sea, and would have passed by them. But when they saw him walking upon the sea, they supposed it had been a spirit, and cried out: For they all saw him, and were troubled. And immediately he talked with them, and saith unto them, Be of good cheer: it is I; be not afraid. And he went up unto them into the ship; and the wind ceased: and they were sore amazed in themselves beyond measure, and wondered. For they considered not the miracle of the loaves: for their heart was hardened.*"

Notice at the beginning of this passage that Jesus made them get in the boat and go ahead of Him. Jesus then watched the disciples strain against the oars because the wind was against them. The Scripture says that later that night, Jesus watched them and waited until shortly before dawn before intervening. A test of faith will bring storms where the winds are against you and you strain in the process, not even considering the loaves. The loaves refer to Jesus feeding the five thousand with five loaves and two fish. This is the evidence the disciples previously witnessed, demonstrating that even the laws of nature and creation are subject to His authority.

The Scripture asserts that the disciples' hearts were hardened, preventing them from understanding. This is to help us learn from their hardened hearts. Observe that while Jesus navigated the turbulent waters, He was on the verge of passing by them. If we are not careful, we will miss Jesus walking past us in the midst of our storms. When the disciples saw Jesus, they didn't recognize Him and thought He was a ghost. In the storm, can you discern Jesus? Or does He appear to you as a ghost that terrifies you? Have you considered the sacrifices He has made in front of your eyes, or have your hearts become hardened?

I can remember the things Jesus has done for me, as well as the miracles in my life. However, during turbulent times, my heart becomes hardened, preventing me from remembering that everything is under His control. During these times, I find myself straining against the wind, not considering the loaves. Like the Disciples, I can feel at times that the storms have become too much to bear, and instead of seeing Jesus in the midst of the storm, I mistake Him for a ghost and am overcome with fear. It's in these situations that I've come to be more disciplined about what I say out of fear and doubt. Some storms may obscure Jesus to such an extent that we lose hope and doubt His continued control. Let the words of Jesus to His disciples speak to us today, and take courage! It is me. Do not be afraid.

The disciples felt God's peace as they witnessed Jesus calm the storm. The Disciples missed the knowledge of God by failing to consider the loaves, even in the midst of the storm. Jesus, knowing He must lay down His life, was preparing the disciples for a time when He wouldn't physically be with them. It's about being able to utilize the Holy Spirit and your spiritual authority through faith in Him. Jesus admonished His disciples time and again, asking them, Where is your faith? Let us not fail to see the lesson Jesus was teaching His disciples. To please God, we must demonstrate our faith through our words.

Hebrews 11:6 says, *"And without faith, it is impossible to please God, because anyone who comes to Him must believe that He exists and that He rewards those who earnestly seek Him."* Romans 10:10 states, *"You believe and receive justification with your heart, and you profess your faith and receive salvation with your mouth."* We profess our faith by speaking it; we speak it because we believe it in our hearts. The question is: what do we have stored up in our hearts? Jesus speaks of these things when describing a tree and its fruit.

Luke 6:43–45 says, *"No good tree bears bad fruit, and neither does a bad tree bear good fruit. We recognize each tree by its own fruit. People do not pick figs from thorn bushes or grapes from briers. A beneficial man brings good things out of the good stored up in his heart, and an evil man brings evil things out of the evil stored up in his heart. For the mouth speaks what the heart is full of."* This teaching of Jesus takes on a different light for us as believers who live our lives without much thought of what words we are speaking in times of trouble. The storms we face are an opportunity to express faith stored in our hearts. Has Jesus done enough for you in your life that you can consider the loaves in times of trouble? Consider the loaves in your life. Then speak and express your faith, which is both the substance of things hoped for and evidence of things not seen. Speak the truth of God stored up in your heart to the factual elements of your storm and watch His Word come alive in you.

Mark 11:12-14 says, *"The next day, as they were leaving Bethany, Jesus was hungry. Seeing in the distance a fig tree in leaf, He went to find out if it had any fruit. When He reached it, He found nothing but leaves, because it was not the season for figs. Then He said to the tree, May no one ever eat fruit from you again. And His disciples heard Him say it."* What did the fig tree do to Jesus? The Scripture says it wasn't the season for figs. Why would Jesus curse a fig tree that was only doing what it could do in its particular season? The last sentence provides the answer, as Jesus demonstrated this to His disciples. The fig tree was in the leaf stage with a fruity appearance. However, the disciples were getting ready to spread the gospel. 2 Timothy 4:2 says, *"Preach the Word; be prepared in season and out of season; correct, rebuke, and encourage—with great patience and careful instruction."*

Jesus, in His infinite wisdom, was speaking through His actions of truth to not only His disciples walking with Him then but to us today as well. We should be fruitful, both in and out of season. We should not be like the fig tree, which is limited in its fruiting season. Though it had leaves, it had no fruit, as Jesus further explains in Mark 11:20-24, *"In the morning, as they went along, they saw the fig tree wither from its roots. Peter remembered and said to Jesus, Rabbi, look! The fig tree you cursed has withered! 'Have faith in God', Jesus answered. Truly, I tell you, if anyone says to this mountain, "Go throw yourself into the sea," and does not harbor any doubts in their hearts, but believes that what they say will happen, it will indeed come to pass. Therefore, I tell you, whatever you ask for in prayer, believe that you have received it, and it will be yours."*

What a beautiful illustration of spiritual truth! Jesus is drawing a comparison between the fig tree, which has limitations, and us, as believers, who have no limitations. If we choose to live with limitations, bearing only leaves without any fruit due to a lack of faith to ask and believe, we are destined to follow the path of the fig tree. We are given authority through faith. Do we believe this to be true? An evil spirit confronts Jesus in Mark, chapter 9. The man explains how the evil spirit tortures his son and tells Jesus that he asked Jesus' disciples to drive out the spirit, but they could not. Then Jesus responded.

Mark 9:19 says, *"You unbelieving generation, Jesus replied. How long will I stay with you? How long shall I put up with you? Bring the boy to me."* Jesus doesn't hide his frustration at the unbelief, but the man admits something powerful in the midst of it that still speaks today. Mark 9:22-24 says, *"And oftentimes it hath cast him into the fire, and into the waters, to destroy him: but if thou canst do any thing, have compassion on us, and help us. Jesus said unto him, If thou canst believe, all things are possible to him that believeth. And straightway the father of the child cried out, and said with tears, Lord, I believe; help thou mine unbelief."*

42

In such an unbelieving generation, this should be our prayer as believers. "Lord, I do believe. Help me overcome my unbelief." This expression of faith from the boy's father was what it took for Jesus to deliver him from the unclean spirit. Believing the words of Jesus requires faith. Do you truly believe His words? You may say you do believe, but... If this is your response, then you should pray the prayer of the boy's father. Lord, I do believe you can help me overcome my unbelief. Next, apply the principles of belief and begin to express faith through the words you speak.

5

Garden Of Gethsemane

Mark 14:32–42 says, *"And they came to a place which was named Gethsemane: and he saith to his disciples, Sit ye here, while I shall pray. And he taketh with him Peter and James and John, and began to be sore amazed, and to be very heavy; And saith unto them, My soul is exceeding sorrowful unto death: tarry ye here, and watch. And he went forward a little, and fell on the ground, and prayed that, if it were possible, the hour might pass from him. And he said, Abba, Father, all things are possible unto thee; take away this cup from me: nevertheless not what I will, but what thou wilt. And he cometh, and findeth them sleeping, and saith unto Peter, Simon, sleepest thou? couldest not thou watch one hour? Watch ye and pray, lest ye enter into temptation. The spirit truly is ready, but the flesh is weak. And again he went away, and prayed, and spake the same words. And when he returned, he found them asleep again, (for their eyes were heavy,) and neither wist they what to answer him. And he cometh the third time, and saith unto them, Sleep on now, and take your rest: it is enough, the hour is come; behold, the Son of man is betrayed into the hands of sinners. Rise up, let us go; lo, he that betrayeth me is at hand."*

The Garden of Gethsemane is a garden located on a place known as the Mount of Olives. Gethsemane comes from the Hebrew word Gat-Shemanim, which means "oil press." In biblical times, people used the press as a tool to forcefully crush and extract the juice from grapes, or in this case, the oil from olives. In the oil press, there were two major steps. First, we would collect the olives and place them in a vat. Then, they would roll a large stone over the olives to crush them. Next, they would collect the crushed olives into a basket. Then, using a lever and the stone, they would apply pressure to the crushed olives to extract all the remaining oil from the olives. The oil would run out of the basket and into the vat. A crushing stone and a pressing device were integral parts of oil presses. In more modern times, heat and high pressure are more effective. Oil is representative of the anointing of God all throughout the Scriptures. Prophets would pour oil over the heads of kings, symbolizing their anointing as kings.

Understanding the symbolism of oil and realizing that Jesus' experience in Gethsemane resembles an oil press is crucial for comprehending this Scripture. Jesus' experience at Gethsemane provides us with a wealth of information that still holds relevance today. Jesus is the Word of God made flesh. John 1:14 says, *"The Word became flesh and made His dwelling among us. We have seen His glory—the glory of the one and only Son, who came from the Father, full of grace and truth."* Jesus, being the Word of God, made flesh to fulfill God's spoken word through the prophets and documented it in Scripture. The fulfillment of prophecy must occur in and through Jesus. He is the Word of God. Jesus, also made flesh, experienced temptation, pain, emotions, and feelings. It's the made-flesh part of Jesus on display at Gethsemane, not as a sign of weakness in Jesus but as an example to us as fleshly beings and full of His Spirit. The Spirit is willing, but the flesh is weak.

Jesus in Gethsemane was deeply troubled, and He said my soul was overwhelmed with sorrow to the point of death. The made-flesh part of Jesus sought to have the cup of His suffering taken from Him. Remember, Jesus is the Word made flesh. The Word of God cannot return void. The flesh will seek to change the Word of God. This is not Jesus being weak; Jesus fulfilled His Word and set the example for us as fleshly beings in the struggle to submit to obedience to the Word. Hebrews 5:7-9 says, " *Who in the days of his flesh, when he had offered up prayers and supplications with strong crying and tears unto him that was able to save him from death, and was heard in that he feared; Though he were a Son, yet learned he obedience by the things which he suffered; And being made perfect, he became the author of eternal salvation unto all them that obey him.*"

Jesus, being the Word made flesh, had to learn obedience to Himself against His flesh to fulfill Himself as the Word of God. It is not my will, the will of the made flesh, but Your will, the spoken word about Himself. Jesus never denied the cross or rejected His purpose of reconciling the world to God through Himself. This was His purpose. His learning of obedience required him to subordinate His fleshly will to His purpose. That meant coming face-to-face with temptations, emotions, feelings, pain, love, anger, frustrations, and everything concerning the flesh. This is God's mercy that Jesus is able to relate to us and gives us His grace.

Hebrews 2:14-18 states, " *Forasmuch then as the children are partakers of flesh and blood, he also himself likewise took part of the same; that through death he might destroy him that had the power of death, that is, the devil; And deliver them who through fear of death were all their lifetime subject to bondage. For verily he took not on him the nature of angels; but he took on him the seed of Abraham. Wherefore in all things it behoved him to be made like unto his brethren, that he might be a merciful and faithful high priest in things pertaining to God, to make reconciliation for the sins of the people. For in that he himself hath suffered being tempted, he is able to succour them that are tempted.*"

The oil press, or Gethsemane, is required to learn obedience. Sometimes, the strengthening of God brings about anguish and uncomfortable times, creating an urgency of obedience to fulfill His Word and purpose for your life. Your anointing occurs during the most challenging moments of your life. Great crushing yields great anointing. The crushing and subsequent pressing lead to the oil's leakage and storage. 1 Peter 4:12–13 says, *"Beloved, think it not strange concerning the fiery trial which is to try you, as though some strange thing happened unto you: But rejoice, inasmuch as ye are partakers of Christ's sufferings; that, when his glory shall be revealed, ye may be glad also with exceeding joy."*

Like the Disciples in the Garden of Gethsemane, our eyes get heavy, and we often go to sleep during these times. Jesus warned Peter to watch and pray that he would not fall into temptation during this time. It's the battle between our fleshly will and the purpose of God for our lives. Jesus set the example in Gethsemane. We can empathize with others who are grappling with our origins, just as Jesus, tempted in every manner, was able to understand our weakness. The anointing and calling of God in our lives will transform what the devil intended to destroy us into a tool for good. The former addict, who is familiar with that temptation, is able to empathize with the one who is still struggling and needs guidance. Having come from an abusive background, the individual can equip and comfort those experiencing similar situations.

2 Corinthians 1:3-5 says, *"Blessed be God, even the Father of our Lord Jesus Christ, the Father of mercies, and the God of all comfort; Who comforteth us in all our tribulation, that we may be able to comfort them which are in any trouble, by the comfort wherewith we ourselves are comforted of God. For as the sufferings of Christ abound in us, so our consolation also aboundeth by Christ."* Without doubt, the adversity Jesus delivered you from shapes the comfort you can provide to others. The equipping process from which you gain wisdom can often come with its own setbacks and failures. It is in these times that we gain the experience of what God will use through you in the future. It won't make sense at the time, but in hindsight, you will see the workings of God

through the storm. Remember, in the storm, Jesus appeared to be a ghost to the disciples?

I'm not suggesting that God is tempting you. I'm telling you that God is able to use what the devil means to harm you and turn it for your good. If you submit your life to God, I know that a great crushing can bring anointing. When I graduated high school, I went to work at different jobs and sold marijuana on the side. I used to smoke weed daily, and at that time, Oxycontin was a popular drug. I developed an addiction to pain pills and Xanax and occasionally indulged in alcohol. As time went on, my addiction became increasingly severe. It was in 1999 that I began dating my daughter's mother. When she became pregnant in the spring of 2000, I attempted to clean up my life, but it didn't last long.

After she became pregnant, she stopped using drugs, and I began renovating a trailer to provide us with a place to live. Methamphetamine became available to me during this period. I started both selling and using methamphetamine during this period. After my daughter was born on Christmas Eve of 2000, me and her mother were using meth regularly. We were young and not aware of the drug's effects or what it was doing to our bodies. My parents painfully watched the effects taking place and often tried to help us. I was in that phase of blindness where I didn't want to see any other way than what I was doing.

We lived in a two-bedroom trailer out in the woods of Walker County, Alabama. After prolonged use of the drug, we would go days without eating or sleeping. During these times, we would get paranoid, thinking someone was in the woods out to get us. We lived like what you would call functioning addicts. We had jobs, and when we were home, we would get high. There were times we would get so paranoid after being up so long that we would sit in the living room, looking out of the window behind the couch towards the woods where the driveway was. We'd see who we thought was in the woods with a flashlight. The object would disappear, and no further action would occur. This happened on several different occasions.

We were at home the night of February 16, 2002, and had been up for days. As the night progressed to the early morning hours, we became paranoid and thought we saw someone in the woods with a flashlight. Our daughter was in the back bedroom, asleep. She was about 14 months old at the time. We took our original spot propped up on the back of the couch, looking through the blinds towards the woods, where we thought a light flashed, thinking someone was out there. While we were watching, it looked like we saw someone at the edge of the wood line squatting low to the ground. I went and got my gun, which I brought to our living room. We turned off the lights in the trailer and kept watching through the window.

I can't remember how much time passed, but after observing through the window for a while, it appeared as though someone was running along the driveway towards a barn at an angle from the trailer. I told her to go to the back bedroom, where our daughter was sleeping. After she left, I strained to see through the blinds on the side of the trailer. I could feel my heart pounding, and I was filled with fear, unsure of what to do. We didn't have a phone at the trailer back then, and the only way to get a signal on a cell phone was to drive down towards the main highway. I was looking around, trying to see if I could see anyone. I heard a clicking noise. When I heard it again, I tried to look down the side of the trailer.

I grabbed my gun and went down the hallway with my back against the wall. When I came to the middle bedroom, I heard what I thought was the blinds moving and someone coming through the window. I turned into the doorway and fired three shots at the window. I heard a drop, stepped back, and turned on the light. Upon seeing my daughter's mother squatting at the window, I realized I had accidentally shot her. I remembered dropping the gun and running to her, but she was dead. In 2006, they charged me with murder, found me guilty, and sentenced me to life in prison. I did not want to live; I hated myself. For over a decade, I couldn't even talk about it, and I was miserable.

My actions resulted in the shedding of innocent blood, a topic that remains painful to discuss even today. I understand the pain my actions inflicted, and I've often wondered if I could have taken a different course of action that could have resulted in a different outcome. I understand that this tragedy devastated the people it affected, and I bear the responsibility. No one hated me more than I hated myself, I can assure you. I spent the next decade in prison hating myself, torn between trying to defend myself on appeal for an accident and giving up on life altogether. My family believed in me when no one else did, and I'm grateful. My trial was horrible. There were only three of us present at the trial. Witnesses took the stand at my trial, saying things that were not true and trying to get me convicted.

Years later, these witnesses have come forward to confess that they lied during the trial and received payment to do so in order to secure my conviction. The courts would do nothing. In 2016, I found myself in a lockup cell, completely exhausted by life. I was addicted to drugs and had no hope or vision for the future. In that cell, I cried out to Jesus for help. I prayed with my whole heart and wept. I conveyed to God that I am aware of His knowledge of my heart, the events that transpired, and everything else. I fervently prayed for His intervention in my life, accepting the possibility of my death in prison, as He is aware of the truth. I poured it out for God. In that cell, I felt the most peace I had ever felt, and all I could do was weep.

I flushed the drugs down the toilet and began reading the Word of God. I read and learned about Him. I felt an unexplainable peace, and since then I've had ups and downs, setbacks, and failures, but He's never left my side, and I know He is with me. God began to give me a vision and show me a life, and for the first time, I felt I had something to live for. I learned about spiritual warfare and the enemy's deceptive tactics, and it hit me hard. As I grew in the Word of God, opportunities opened up for me to begin speaking at services. I used to never want to stand in front of people and speak, yet now it comes naturally.

I didn't graduate from a university with a degree in theology, but I know I have the Spirit of God in me. I'm thankful to Jesus; He truly saved my life, and I will tell of His miraculous work until my last breath and preach His Word as long as I live. I share this part of my life and past to demonstrate the work He has done in my life, and the Biblical insight I share is a reflection of what He has given me. I am familiar with the process of crushing and pressing oil, as well as the anointing of God. My life without Jesus is nonexistent, but He's shown me that He is life.

There are a lot of things I wish I would have done differently in the past. What is a person to do about things they cannot change? Jesus in Gethsemane felt the pressure, and although His flesh cried out to take the cup from Him, He submitted to the will of the Father. Because Jesus is able to empathize with our struggle and is faithful in His love towards us, the fact that while we were yet sinners, He died for us means everything to me. It's a comforting truth that I cherish. No matter what people have to say about you, He loves you, and even when it is your fault, He is there. What an awesome God we serve!

Psalms 139:7-8 says, "*Whither shall I go from thy spirit? or whither shall I flee from thy presence? If I ascend up into heaven, thou art there: if I make my bed in hell, behold, thou art there.”* The lesson of learned obedience that Jesus portrays in Gethsemane is still being Because of Him, flawed people like me and you have hope and life.d life in Him. His promise to never leave you or forsake you still stands.

6

The War Is Real

2 Corinthians 4:4 says, *"The god of this age has blinded the minds of unbelievers, so that they cannot see the light of the gospel that displays the glory of Christ, who is the image of God."* The devil's deceptive nature preys on young minds to gratify the flesh. In doing so, the devil influences the minds of those who are in a position to advertise these temptations. By using this tactic to poison the minds of numerous individuals, the devil can then prey on the minds of those who share similar temptations, fostering a culture that not only accepts but also condones such behavior. The process of blinding the mind involves presenting temptations in increasingly numerous and distinct ways so that individuals are enticed to succumb to them and acquire knowledge of both good and evil.

However, the tasting of the fruit will twist their concept of good and evil into thinking evil is good. This is the deception. The temporary pleasures of sin will blind the mind to the reality of what the wages of sin bring, which is death. But the gift of God is eternal life in Christ Jesus, our Lord." The same deceptions are active today in more numerous and distinguished forms, similar to what Moses experienced. Moses was born at a time when Pharaoh had issued a decree to kill all the Hebrew boys.

Exodus 1:22 says, *"Then Pharaoh gave this order to all his people: Every Hebrew boy that is born you must throw into the Nile, but let every girl live."* So Moses was born, and his parents hid him for three months. They then placed him in a basket and put him along the reeds of the Nile. Pharaoh's daughter discovered Moses, was full of compassion, and took him in. Pharaoh's daughter then sought to get a Hebrew woman to nurse him. God's favor made it possible for Moses to receive nursing care from his own mother and receive compensation in return. Pharaoh's daughter then adopted Moses and raised him in the king's palace. As Moses grew up, he had a choice to make, as did we all.

Hebrews 11:23-27 says, *"By faith Moses, when he was born, was hid three months of his parents, because they saw he was a proper child; and they were not afraid of the king's commandment. By faith Moses, when he was come to years, refused to be called the son of Pharaoh's daughter; Choosing rather to suffer affliction with the people of God, than to enjoy the pleasures of sin for a season; Esteeming the reproach of Christ greater riches than the treasures in Egypt: for he had respect unto the recompence of the reward. By faith he forsook Egypt, not fearing the wrath of the king: for he endured, as seeing him who is invisible."*

The god of this age has issued an edict that aims to destroy our youth. He does so by deceiving them and enticing them with an evil culture that believes evil is good and acceptable. Many of us, like Moses, have parents or loved ones who were full of faith and prayed for us to not be afraid of the issued edict. Moses grew up in a culture of sin and fleeting pleasures. Moses realized that the treasures of Egypt paled in comparison to his reward because he had a clear vision. In the midst of his circumstances, Moses made a choice by faith that the temporary pleasures of sin were not worth it.

Today, it is evident that the war is real. Whether it's broken homes, various addictions, enticing lust, greed, or anything else influencing your mind that drives you every day, the war is real. We have an enemy whose sole purpose is to steal, kill, and destroy you. This enemy targets not just you, but also all your possessions and personal details. Think about your life and the circumstances that have shaped it. You were born to parents that you did not choose, in a situation and circumstance completely out of your control. People you had no control over raised you, teaching you ways of life you were unaware of. As a child, you observed others' actions and assimilated their behavior, influenced by what they learned or experienced in their own lives.

As you mature, you start making independent decisions based on what you've been taught and observed, often oblivious to the power of influence working against you. You also make your own mistakes and poor choices. When you consider that you have an enemy, unknown to you, who seeks to destroy you from the womb, it becomes clear that not only is he your enemy, but also all of creation. You then realize the need for a Savior. This realization is exactly what the enemy is trying to blind you to see. Every situation is unique with countless invariable but this truth applies to everyone.

Once you recognize this truth, the deception will try to persuade you to believe in anything other than the One True Savior, Jesus. Often, life can plunge a person into a deep abyss, leaving them with no other choice but to turn to God. Then, in that distressed time, you call out to Him with your whole heart and truly believe in Him because you finally realize there are no other options. At this point, the war takes a different approach but is still very real. The difference now is that you have power through Him to overcome. The Word of God gives us instructions on how to fight in this war.

Ephesians 6:13-17 says, *"Therefore, put on the full armor of God, so that when the day of evil comes, you may be able to stand your ground, and after you have done everything to stand. Stand firm, then, with the belt of truth buckled around your waist, the breastplate of righteousness in place, and your feet fitted with the readiness that comes from the gospel of peace. In addition to all this, take up the shield of faith, with which you can extinguish all the flaming arrows of the evil one. Take the helmet of salvation and the sword of the Spirit, which is the Word of God."* First, it is important to note in this Scripture that you put on God's full armor so that when the day of evil comes, you may be able to stand your ground. And after you have done everything to stand up, stand firm. The armor of God provides a comprehensive guide for preparing for spiritual warfare.

One of the biggest mistakes and outlooks a new believer can have is thinking that since they received Jesus as their Lord and Savior, attacks will stop coming. God has called you, designed you for a unique purpose, and given you gifts and talents to do good works that glorify Him. This is why attacks keep coming, and it is important to have the belt of truth buckled around your waist. If you buckle half-truths around your waist, then the attacks will overtake you. You grow weary and faint. It's important that you read God's Word and learn His truth about you.

1 Peter 2:2–3 says, *"Like newborn babies, crave pure spiritual milk so that you may grow up in your salvation after tasting that the Lord is good."* Learn about your position and claim it. 1 Peter 2:9–10 also puts it like this, *"But you are a chosen people, a royal priesthood, a holy nation, God's special possession, that you may declare the prayers of Him who called you out of darkness into His wonderful light."* Once you were not a people, but now you are the people of God. Once you had not received mercy, but now you have received mercy." The enemy's attack will attempt to discredit this truth about you by making you feel condemned by your shortcomings or failures. The devil will use

everything at his disposal to make you condemn yourself.

The story of Balaam illustrates the enemies' attempts to curse what God has blessed. Although he is incapable of doing so, he can persuade you to carry out the curse yourself. How? He manipulates you into feeling undeserving, leading you to succumb to his cunning tactics. Then, placing the lies of your unworthiness in your mind, you speak curses over your own life. Instead of buckling your waist with God's truth, you exchange it for a lie. Romans 1:21-25 says, *"Because that, when they knew God, they glorified him not as God, neither were thankful; but became vain in their imaginations, and their foolish heart was darkened. Professing themselves to be wise, they became fools, And changed the glory of the uncorruptible God into an image made like to corruptible man, and to birds, and fourfooted beasts, and creeping things. Wherefore God also gave them up to uncleanness through the lusts of their own hearts, to dishonour their own bodies between themselves: Who changed the truth of God into a lie, and worshipped and served the creature more than the Creator, who is blessed for ever. Amen."*

Without the buckle of truth around your waist, you will fall for the enemy's lies. The vision you received from God, which appears to have not yet materialized, will indeed come to pass. Stand Firm. By faith, speak life over it. Do the work with your hands, and He will give you the increase. The enemy's lies will attempt to discourage you and place unworthy thoughts in your mind. Claim your victory in Jesus name. Speak His truth to the facts the enemy has laid before you. Stand your ground and buckle His truth around your waist. When thoughts of failure infiltrate your mind, exercise your authority and allow Jesus to cleanse your temple courts, even as the enemy tries to deceive you.

Build your relationship with Jesus and walk with Him. He is your breastplate of righteousness. Without cultivating your relationship with Jesus and becoming personally acquainted with Him, you will try to justify yourself by your righteousness. Therefore, it's out of place. The Bible instructs us to put on the armor of righteousness. The spirit of comparison is a lie that the enemy tries to use against the truth. They should have chosen you for this position. You are more qualified. This attempt at misplacing your breastplate is a tactic to cause division and conflict. Keep your buckle of truth fastened in these times, and those attempts will fall short. Our righteousness is like a filthy rag, and it is only in Jesus' righteousness that we stand.

Isaiah 64:6 says, *"But we are all as an unclean thing, and all our righteousness are as filthy rags; and we all do fade as a leaf; and our iniquities, like the wind, have taken us away."* When you understand the truth of God, wear the belt of truth around your waist, and secure the breastplate of righteousness, the gospel of peace will equip your feet with the readiness it brings. It's God's peace with this armor properly intact that makes us ready to share the good news. Being a faithful witness to God's work in your life, you are a living testament to His grace, mercy, and unfailing love.

Revelation 12:11 says, *"They triumphed over him with the blood of the lamb, and by the word of their testimony, they did not love their lives so much as to shrink from death."* In the Book of John, Jesus is disputing with some unbelieving Jews over who their Father is. John 8:31-47 says, *"Then said Jesus to those Jews which believed on him, If ye continue in my word, then are ye my disciples indeed; And ye shall know the truth, and the truth shall make you free. They answered him, We be Abraham's seed, and were never in bondage to any man: how sayest thou, Ye shall be made free? Jesus answered them, Verily, verily, I say unto you, Whosoever committeth sin is the servant of sin. And the servant abideth not in the house for ever: but the Son abideth ever. If the Son therefore shall make you free, ye shall be free indeed. I know that ye are Abraham's seed; but ye seek to kill me, because my word hath no place in you. I speak that which I have seen with my Father: and ye do that which ye have seen with your father. They answered and said unto him,*

Abraham is our father. Jesus saith unto them, If ye were Abraham's children, ye would do the works of Abraham. But now ye seek to kill me, a man that hath told you the truth, which I have heard of God: this did not Abraham. Ye do the deeds of your father. Then said they to him, We be not born of fornication; we have one Father, even God. Jesus said unto them, If God were your Father, ye would love me: for I proceeded forth and came from God; neither came I of myself, but he sent me. Why do ye not understand my speech? even because ye cannot hear my word. Ye are of your father the devil, and the lusts of your father ye will do. He was a murderer from the beginning, and abode not in the truth, because there is no truth in him. When he speaketh a lie, he speaketh of his own: for he is a liar, and the father of it. And because I tell you the truth, ye believe me not. Which of you convinceth me of sin? And if I say the truth, why do ye not believe me? He that is of God heareth God's words: ye therefore hear them not, because ye are not of God."

Jesus said that you would know the truth, and the truth would set you free. The truth is that the belt we buckle around our waist holds the breastplate of righteousness in place. This truth is constantly under attack in our lives. The father of lies tries to persuade you into exchanging God's truth for a lie. What does God's Word say about who you are in Him? 2 Corinthians 5:18–21 says, *"And all things are of God, who hath reconciled us to himself by Jesus Christ, and hath given to us the ministry of reconciliation; To wit, that God was in Christ, reconciling the world unto himself, not imputing their trespasses unto them; and hath committed unto us the word of reconciliation. Now then we are ambassadors for Christ, as though God did beseech you by us: we pray you in Christ's stead, be ye reconciled to God. For he hath made him to be sin for us, who knew no sin; that we might be made the righteousness of God in him."*

You must know your identity in Christ. Despite the enemy's lies and the fiery darts that attack your mind, the shield of faith will quench them. Your words express your faith. Confession leads to salvation through the mouth. With your mouth, you speak either God's truth about you or the lies that the enemy attacks you with. The tongue contains the power of life and death. Every morning you must speak your identity in Christ Jesus. The armor of God is our protection. The belt of truth is vital; if you fail to claim your identity in Christ, you are vulnerable to accepting the lie. If you exchange God's truth for a lie, you will follow the will of the father of lies. Instead of being an ambassador for Christ, you will express your fears and doubts. Your words will become a snare to your soul.

You are God's righteousness through Jesus. Claim it. You are God's temple. Claim it. The enemy's lies had convinced me long enough that my life was over. I would never be anything. I used to believe everything negative that the devil could conjure up about me. The pit that Jesus rescued me from was a low one, devoid of hope. It was a valley of dry bones. Fear, confusion, doubt, and negativity drove my outlook. My words matched my life, and they took me to a place where I cried out to Jesus. Throughout my walk with Jesus, I've diligently sought His understanding of His Word and how to apply His truths to my life. Claiming my identity every morning has proven vital to my outlook throughout the day.

2 Corinthians 4:16 says, *"Therefore, we do not lose heart. Despite our outward deterioration, we experience daily renewal within."* The Helmet of Salvation is my security, protecting my mind. I am confident that Christ Jesus, who laid down His life for me and rose again to grant me existence, is the source of my salvation. Jesus assures me of eternal life, regardless of the circumstances of this life. Growing in His Word and knowing Him personally, He equips you with the sword of the Spirit, which is His Word.

Isaiah 54:17 says, *"No weapon formed against you will prevail, and you will refute every tongue that accuses you. This is the heritage of the servants of the Lord, and this is their vindication from Me, declares the Lord."* The weapons will be formed against you. They can appear deadly and intimidating. According to God's Word, they will not prevail. The Lord promises to refute every tongue that accuses you. He doesn't promise that no one will accuse you. This scripture serves as a battleground for speaking truth to a factual circumstance and wielding the sword of the Spirit. The Word of God bestows upon us beautiful promises. Do we believe in them? Do we speak them, or are our words reflective of the enemy's lies?

Faith is to be tested. There were times I thought, in my understanding, that God was going to make a way for me. When it didn't happen, I seriously questioned God. There were times I angrily talked to God and poured out my heart in frustration. The denial of parole hurt me deeply. After completing numerous classes, I believed I had done enough to earn another chance at life. I've served more than 21 years in prison, and I harbor visions of a ministry known as the Outpouring Ministry. I am aware of what God has revealed to me, and I am confident in His presence. It is painful when I lose what seems like my chance. When this happened in the past, I would spiral into depressive thoughts and face powerful attacks. I would feel that God had failed me. I would boldly go to the Throne of Grace and seek understanding. I would feel peace, but I lacked discipline, and I would have a negative mindset.

Overwhelmed by fear and doubt, I would seek life and converse with death. I recall dialing home and hearing my parents sob, perplexed by my rejection. They would tell me that God has a plan and that I should trust Him. When I put my trust in Him, who knows the truth, I understand the pain of a closed door and the feeling of denial. It hurts. I also know that His words are true. Although I may have a tendency to rely on my own understanding when I believe God should have done something, this can lead to doubts that the devil can exploit. While I have a vision of a ministry when I am free, I also have the opportunity to minister here.

Through the denials and setbacks, I've grown closer to Jesus, and I've witnessed God use what was meant for my harm for my good. I've talked about writing a book for the past several years but never got past that talking stage. I would put it off, promising to write it when the circumstances were more favorable or after my release. I'm writing this book not from an air-conditioned office in the comfort of home but from prison, where I'm in the midst of my struggle and leaning on the promises of God's Word myself. Truth be told, I'm having a good time with the Lord during the process. The circumstances are not favorable, but the grace of God is sufficient even in this.

Whatever your current situation may be, keep trusting in Him, who is able to deliver you. You cannot go wrong if you put your complete trust in Jesus. We know that spiritual warfare is real. I was unaware of how seriously it affected me every day. I pray that the Holy Spirit will guide and comfort you by relating these truths to your own life. Listen to Him and seek Him with your whole heart.

7

Anointed Not Yet Appointed

TRUST THE PROCESS

1 Thessalonians 5:16–24 says, *"Rejoice always, pray continually, and give thanks in all circumstances; for this is God's will for you in Christ Jesus." Do not quench the Spirit. Do not treat prophecies with contempt, but test them all, hold onto what is good, and reject every kind of evil. May God Himself, the God of Peace, sanctify you through and through. May the coming of our Lord Jesus Christ keep your whole spirit, soul, and body blameless. "The one who calls you is faithful, and he will do it."*

One reason people struggle to trust the process is that they confuse God's anointing with His appointment. King David serves as a major example of this truth. David had the anointing to be king, but he hadn't yet been appointed. In fact, David did not take the throne until approximately 14 years after his anointing. Before David's appointment could come to pass, certain events and circumstances had to occur in his life. God's anointing ensures the fulfillment of the promise. The process brings forth the promise.

While the anointing serves as an assurance of the promise, it is also your responsibility to persevere through the process until the work within and for you is complete. Preparation is key throughout this process. If you are properly prepared and seize your opportunity, you will achieve success. In the Book of 1 Samuel, the Israelites requested to have a king rule over them like other nations. 1 Samuel 8:4–7 says, *"Then all the elders of Israel gathered themselves together, and came to Samuel unto Ramah, And said unto him, Behold, thou art old, and thy sons walk not in thy ways: now make us a king to judge us like all the nations. But the thing displeased Samuel, when they said, Give us a king to judge us. And Samuel prayed unto the Lord. And the Lord said unto Samuel, Hearken unto the voice of the people in all that they say unto thee: for they have not rejected thee, but they have rejected me, that I should not reign over them."*

The Lord directed Samuel to anoint Saul as King of Israel. The Scriptures say that Saul was 30 years old when he became king and reigned for 42 years. Saul began to disobey the Word of God, and ultimately God rejected Saul. In 1 Samuel 15:10-11, it states, *"Then the Word of the Lord came to Samuel: I regret that I made Saul king, because he has turned away from me and has not carried out my instructions. Samuel was angry, and he cried out all that night."* 1 Samuel 16:1 says,*"And the Lord said unto Samuel, How long wilt thou mourn for Saul, seeing I have rejected him from reigning over Israel? fill thine horn with oil, and go, I will send thee to Jesse the Bethlehemite: for I have provided me a king among his sons."*

Samuel went to Bethlehem to visit Jesse's house, and as each of Jesse's sons stood before Samuel, the Lord had not chosen any of them. 1 Samuel 16:11–13 says,*"He asked Jesse, 'Are these all the sons that you have?'" Jesse replied, "There is still the youngest son." He is tending the sheep. Samuel said, Send him; we will not sit down until he arrives. So he sent for him and had him brought in. He was in good health, had a fine appearance, and had handsome features. Then the Lord said, Rise and anoint him; this is the one. So Samuel took the horn of oil and anointed it in the presence of his brothers, and from that day on, the Spirit of the Lord came powerfully upon David. Samuel then went to Ramah."*

Reading this Scripture would lead one to believe that David would immediately ascend to the throne due to his anointing as king. That is not the case. Despite David's anointing as king, his official appointment was still pending. Some things had to happen first. David became a talented musician, along with tending the sheep. God gave David the talents he would need for his appointment as king to come to fruition. David, not immediately ascending to the throne after his anointing, could have lost hope. He could have grown bitter and full of doubt. He was just a shepherd boy, the youngest of his brothers. As the years passed, David might have thought, "It seems God would've done it by now."

Instead of growing bitter, David began to develop his talents. As he developed his talents, his reputation among his peers grew. 1 Samuel 16:14–18 says, *"But the Spirit of the Lord departed from Saul, and an evil spirit from the Lord troubled him. And Saul's servants said unto him, Behold now, an evil spirit from God troubleth thee. Let our lord now command thy servants, which are before thee, to seek out a man, who is a cunning player on an harp: and it shall come to pass, when the evil spirit from God is upon thee, that he shall play with his hand, and thou shalt be well. And Saul said unto his servants, Provide me now a man that can play well, and bring him to me. Then answered one of the servants, and said, Behold, I have seen a son of Jesse the Bethlehemite, that is cunning in playing, and a mighty valiant man, and a man of war, and prudent in matters, and a comely person, and the Lord is with him."*

David has never been in a battle or fought for Israel's army. The attendants of Saul spoke of his reputation as a brave man and a warrior, based on his record of killing a lion and a bear that attacked his father's sheep. David had faith in his anointing. Since the Prophet Samuel anointed David, the Scripture says that the Spirit of the Lord came powerfully upon him. David began to discover talents, and he grew in courage and trust in the Word of the Lord spoken over him through Samuel. The circumstances didn't favor David. His father vetted him, confident one of his older sons would be chosen.

1 Samuel 16:7 says, *"But the Lord said to Samuel, Do not consider his appearance or his height, for I have rejected him. The Lord does not look at the things people see. People look at the outward appearance, but the Lord looks at the heart."* David took the word of the Lord spoken through Samuel over him as truth. Remembering the truth spoken over you will give you courage in fear. A lion and a bear attacked David while he was tending his father's sheep. Knowing who he was by believing in the Word of God, David did not succumb to fear in this situation. The Word of God stated that he was to be King of Israel. David knew that his fate was not in the hands of a lion or a bear. He trusted the Word of the Lord. This seems like reckless behavior on David's part, but God was strengthening him through faith.

David also discovered a talent for using the slingshot. Being undersized and tending the sheep, David knew of the dangers in the wilderness. He developed this talent in such a way that it would pay off handsomely for him. David didn't waste his time doubting what God said. He used his time perfecting the skills that God gave him, trusting that God was faithful and able to do what He said. David was in preparation mode, and it proved vital to his appointment as king. Despite the challenges, David made the most of his resources and, as a result, received even more.

There was a Philistine giant named Goliath, who was a champion of Gath. By all appearances, he was unbeatable, and everyone was terrified of him. For 40 days, Goliath would come out of the camp day after day, intimidating and defying Israel's armies. King Saul sent David to deliver some food to his brothers who were serving in the army. As David was checking on his brothers, he heard Goliath shout his usual defiance and witnessed the Israelites in the army flee in fear of him. 1 Samuel 17:25 says, *"Now the Israelites have been saying, Do you see how this man keeps coming out?" He comes out to defy Israel. The king will give a lot of money to the man who kills him. He will also marry his daughter and exempt his family from taxes in Israel."*

In this moment, David realized that his preparation had been for this opportunity. David did not fear Goliath. David knew how to kill him from a distance, and he was amazed at the lack of faith in the others. This amount of courage took time and experience, and David could truly say the Lord was with me. David speaks of his journey of faith as he addresses King Saul. 1 Samuel 17:34–37 says, *"And David said unto Saul, Thy servant kept his father's sheep, and there came a lion, and a bear, and took a lamb out of the flock: And I went out after him, and smote him, and delivered it out of his mouth: and when he arose against me, I caught him by his beard, and smote him, and slew him. Thy servant slew both the lion and the bear: and this uncircumcised Philistine shall be as one of them, seeing he hath defied the armies of the living God. David said moreover, The Lord that delivered me out of the paw of the lion, and out of the paw of the bear, he will deliver me out of the hand of this Philistine. And Saul said unto David, Go, and the Lord be with thee."*

This journey of trusting in the Word of God spoken over him through Samuel was a process. Just like God was preparing David, He is preparing us today. Trust His Word. David was not a perfect man, and he made many incorrect decisions throughout his life. David trusted God, took Him at His Word, and believed that God was able to do what He promised. David knew that his anointing was a guarantee of the promise to come. Today, we have the promise guaranteed by receiving the Holy Spirit and anointing. The same Spirit that powerfully came upon David and raised Christ from the dead lives in you.

David spoke the truth about God in front of the facts because he was confident. Every lion and bear God has rescued you from is your testimony, strength, and faith that He will succeed again. Do you have the courage to speak this truth or let the enemy's lies create doubt and fear? Jesus expresses these truths in the parables of the growing seed and the mustard seed. Mark 4:26–34 says, *"He also said, "This is what the kingdom of God is like. A man scatters seed on the ground. Night and day, whether he sleeps or gets up, the seed sprouts and grows, though he does not know how. All by itself the soil produces grain—first the stalk, then the head, then the full kernel in the head. As soon as the grain is ripe, he puts the sickle to it, because the harvest has come." Again he said, "What shall we say the kingdom of God is like, or what parable shall we use to describe it? It is like a mustard seed, which is the smallest of all seeds on earth. Yet when planted, it grows and becomes the largest of all garden plants, with such big branches that the birds can perch in its shade." With many similar parables Jesus spoke the word to them, as much as they could understand. He did not say anything to them without using a parable. But when he was alone with his own disciples, he explained everything."*

Jesus compares the Kingdom of God to a man who sows and reaps. The man scatters seeds and does not know how they produce the grain, but when it is time, he understands how to harvest it. So it is with the seeds of our words. Galatians 6:7-8 says, *"Do not be deceived; God cannot be mocked; a man reaps what he sows. Whoever sows to please their flesh, from the flesh will reap destruction; whoever sows to please the Spirit, from the Spirit will reap eternal life."* David successfully progressed through and grew in his trust and faith in the living God, which is why God calls David a man after His own heart.

In Acts 13:22, the Bible says, *"After removing Saul, he made David their king." God testified concerning him: 'I have found David, son of Jesse, a man after My Own Heart; he will do everything I want him to do."* The journey of David from a shepherd boy to defeating Goliath is remarkable. The progress and growth through that time of preparation are the benchmarks for believers in our walk. We deepen our trust and faith in our God, enabling us to conquer every obstacle on our journey, confident in His presence. Knowing that our gifts and talents align with His purpose for our lives, we make use of them.

You might find it difficult to understand at the moment. It may seem like it's all for nothing or just a waste of time. The shield of faith quenches the devil's fiery darts as you wear the armor of God. The enemy wishes to discourage you and tear you down with doubt and fear. He then presents you with temptations of evil desires that you have overcome in order to lure you back into slavery. This is the struggle and testing of faith. In these moments, do you utilize the sword of the Spirit and speak what God says concerning you? I would fail these tests miserably. As soon as something didn't go how I expected it or God didn't move on my behalf like I thought He should have, I would grow weary and faint.

I would express doubt and negativity about myself and my circumstances. How could this happen? Where are you, God? Why are you allowing this to go on? I would be so bold as to accuse God of deserting me. I thought you wouldn't leave me or forsake me, God. I have had moments when I feel like God doesn't exist and everything is pointless. These were tests that I repeatedly failed. When I learned about positive events in other people's lives, I couldn't genuinely rejoice for them, as the deep-rooted resentment in my soul stemmed from a sense of God's disappointment. I would fall repeatedly into the devil's trap. I lost myself in my depressed state of mind, searching for any substance that could provide momentary relief.

Would I bargain with God? Do this for me, and I'll do everything you want. In my heart, I was thirsty for God, and in my mind, the devil wreaked havoc on my thoughts. I cried out over and over again. Lord, help me. He showed me how to use spiritual authority by casting down strongholds and imaginations that the enemy attacked me with, as well as how to cleanse the temple courts. He showed me how to hold these thoughts captive in Christ obedience. He saved me in such a way that I am truly free, and I will live this life for Him. The fact that King David made significant progress in his trust and faith in God, despite his repeated mistakes, instills hope in me. Although God described David as a man after His own heart, his actions today would have led to his imprisonment.

Despite being imprisoned, facing public criticism, and facing cancellation, God remained by his side. Is it anything more than a beautiful display of God's mercy and kindness that gives us such hope? The Lord repeatedly chastened David, but David also recognized God's mercy. After David killed Goliath, Saul became very jealous of David. So much so that Saul tried to kill David multiple times. David had to hide from Saul. Throughout these trying times, David had the opportunity to kill Saul and take the throne, but David held back, saying he could not kill what God had anointed. David understood the power of anointing; he cherished it. Even in a time of fear for his life, he knew the Word of God would prevail.

1 Samuel 26:9–11 says, *"And David said to Abishai, Destroy him not: for who can stretch forth his hand against the Lord's anointed, and be guiltless?" David said furthermore, As the Lord liveth, the Lord shall smite him; or his day shall come to die; or he shall descend into battle, and perish. The Lord forbid that I should stretch forth mine hand against the Lord's anointed; but, I pray thee, take thou now the spear that is at his bolster, and the cruse of water, and let us go."* The faith of David is strong. He has witnessed the progression of God's power play out on his behalf time and again. Instead of thinking in his flesh, even on the run in fear from Saul, David was able to trust that God was with him. This is a powerful example that speaks to us today. We have witnessed the hand of God at work in our lives. David was on the run from Saul, and fear

was with him. But he knew God was with him too. In the face of fear and an opportunity to eliminate the source of his fear in the flesh, David relied on the hand of God instead. Even though Saul fell into God's hands, David recognized God's anointing.

David, sparing Saul's life, still left him feeling vulnerable and afraid. David, fearful and exhausted from fleeing Saul, decided to go to enemy territory. In 1 Samuel 27:1, *"And David said in his heart, I shall now perish one day by the hand of Saul: there is nothing better for me than that I should speedily escape into the land of the Philistines; and Saul shall despair of me, to seek me any more in any coast of Israel: so shall I escape out of his hand."* Notice the difference in David's demeanor and attitude. He had the chance to destroy Saul, and he was full of faith. Now doubt and fear have overcome his thoughts and convinced him to go into enemy territory. This is the outline of the enemy's plan for all of us. To deceive us into enemy territory. This reckless path will always lead us into danger. A temporary reprieve in enemy territory is playing right into the enemy's hands.

Once the devil can get you into a situation like this, he will convince you to turn on your own people, or the people of God. David, upon entering Philistine territory, went to Achish, son of Maok, king of Gath. David dwelt in Gath, where Goliath, whom he had defeated and killed, was from. After a while, Achish gave David a place called Ziklag where he, his men, and their families could live. David lived in this territory for a year and four months. During this time, David raided nearby territories. 1 Samuel 27:9–12 says, *"And David smote the land, and left neither man nor woman alive, and took away the sheep, and the oxen, and the asses, and the camels, and the apparel, and returned, and came to Achish. And Achish said, Whither have ye made a road to day? And David said, Against the south of Judah, and against the south of the Jerahmeelites, and against the south of the Kenites. And David saved neither man nor woman alive, to bring tidings to Gath, saying, Lest they should tell on us, saying, So did*

David, and so will be his manner all the while he dwelleth in the country of the Philistines. And Achish believed David, saying, He hath made his people Israel utterly to abhor him; therefore he shall be my servant for ever."

This illustrates the tendency to rely on one's own understanding rather than seeking guidance from God. During this time, David is not consulting the Lord. He is acting out of fear and doubt, unaware that the enemy's deception has infiltrated his thoughts. Throughout this error, we read that David "thought" instead of what the Lord said. In this error, the enemy thought to himself, "David has become so obnoxious to his people, the Israelites, that he will be my servant for life." This is the enemy's plan for all of us. The enemy aims to instill in us a sense of fear and uncertainty, leading us to bargain with his falsehoods and succumb to the persuasive lies that have crept into our sacred spaces. The enemy's deceptive nature will try to lead us into war against God's people.

1 Samuel 28:1- says, *"In those days, the Philistines gathered their forces to fight against Israel. Achish said to David, You must understand that you and your men will accompany me in the army. David said, Then you will see for yourself what your servant can do. Achish replied, Very well, I will make you my bodyguard for life."* What was previously thought to himself is now spoken over David by Achish. Achish lays a curse on the blessings bestowed by God. Achish told David he would make him his bodyguard for life.

God anointed David as King of Israel. The enemy's plan cannot stand against the Word of God. As David and his men march with Achish and the Philistines, there is confusion amongst the commanders of the Philistine army, and they are fearful that David will turn on them and regain favor with Saul in the middle of the war. 1 Samuel 29:6–9 says, *"Then Achish called David, and said unto him, Surely, as the Lord liveth, thou hast been upright, and thy going out and thy coming in with me in the host is good in my sight: for I have not found evil in thee since the day of thy coming unto me unto this day: nevertheless the lords favour thee not. Wherefore now return, and go in peace, that thou displease not the lords of the Philistines. And David said unto Achish, But what have I done? And what hast thou found in thy servant so long as I have been with thee unto this day, that I may not go fight against the enemies of my lord the king? And Achish answered and said to David, I know that thou art good in my sight, as an angel of God: notwithstanding the princes of the Philistines have said, He shall not go up with us to the battle."*

The mercy of God is a beautiful thing. Even in the midst of error, God is faithful. Despite his zeal, David was blind to his new role and eager to wage war against the people who had anointed him as king. Do not be surprised when you find yourself in error, disrupting what you were attempting to accomplish, and find yourself unable to proceed with a plan that, while seemingly correct, turned out to be wrong. You can't see it in the moment because of blindness, but in hindsight, you will see how God protected you from yourself. During these times, God will use things to get your attention and help you focus back on Him.

1 Samuel 30:3-6 says, *"So David and his men came to the city, and, behold, it was burned with fire; and their wives, and their sons, and their daughters, were taken captives. Then David and the people that were with him lifted up their voice and wept, until they had no more power to weep. And David's two wives were taken captives, Ahinoam the Jezreelitess, and Abigail the wife of Nabal the Carmelite. And David was greatly distressed; for the people spake of stoning him, because the soul of all the people was grieved, every man for his sons and for his daughters: but David encouraged himself in the Lord his God."* We read this and think, "Finally, David came back to his senses." However, when fear and doubt blind us, we fail to see our own mistakes and hastily pass judgment on others. Like David, sometimes it takes a catastrophic situation to bring our attention back to the

Lord. It can take major circumstances in life to make us call out to Jesus.

David understood the source of his strength; he experienced distractions, yet he knew the right path when there was no other option. Trusting the process is what David did best. Even though he made incorrect decisions, he allowed God to complete His work in his heart. Because of his anointment, David didn't rush to his appointment. He allowed God to work in him. It is comforting to us, as flawed human beings, that the grace and mercy of our God endure forever. He is longing for our flaws and forgiving of our shortcomings. He will leave the 99 to go in search of that one. Thank you, Jesus! David asked the Lord if he should pursue the raiding party that had taken their families captive. The Lord said to pursue them; you will certainly overtake them and succeed in the rescue. David and his men rescued their families, and a short time later, Saul died. As predicted, David eventually ascended to the throne. He was 30 years old when he became king, and he reigned for 40 years.

8

He Equips The Called

In Ephesians 4:11-13, the Bible says, *"So Christ Himself gave the Apostles, the Prophets, the Evangelists, the Pastors, and the Teachers to equip His people for works of service so that the Body of Christ may be built up until we all reach unity in the faith and in the knowledge of the Son of God and become mature, attaining to the whole measure of the fullness of Christ."* The most relatable and powerful people who minister the Word of God are those who are open, honest, and transparent about the struggles in their own lives. It's dangerous when one ministers and attempts to give the appearance that they have it all together. The mere act of anointing will trigger an attack from the enemy. This, in and of itself, is part of the equipping process. A man truly seeking God will receive God's wisdom and gain clarity from His Word, which he is to share with the people of God.

James 1:2-8 says, *"Consider it pure joy, my brothers and sisters, whenever you face trials of many types, because you know that the testing of your faith produces perseverance. Let perseverance finish its work so that you are mature and complete, not lacking anything. If any of you lack wisdom, seek it from God, who bestows wisdom generously and without judgment, and you will receive it. But when you ask, you must believe and not doubt, because the one who doubts is like a wave of the sea, blown and tossed by the wind. The person should not expect to receive anything from the Lord. Such a person is double-minded and unstable in all they do."*

When I became a born-again believer in Jesus and witnessed His transformational power at work in my life, I was transferred to a different prison. It was at this prison that I graduated from the Transformational Ministry program. The program, which lasted for a full year, was truly amazing. During this period in my life, I participated in classes and small groups that convened in the chapel every night of the week, which were not affiliated with transformational ministry. Anyone in the prison was welcome to attend these small groups. I'd expect guys who are openly struggling with addictions to attend these classes. We would pray for these men, talk about the Word of God, and discuss spiritual warfare. Some of these guys would attend these classes with high expectations, but they would also openly discuss their struggles. This became a struggle for me. I was a witness to God's power and how He delivered me, so I couldn't understand why they seemed unwilling to change.

As time progressed and these guys continued to attend these classes, discussing their aspirations for change, I found myself observing them in the yard as a group almost every day. I would be with a group of guys from the chapel out on the yard, and I would see these other guys in their struggle, and I would make comments to my friends about it. I began to formulate judgments against them and criticize them for others. I even confronted some of these guys, urging them to cease succumbing to their weaknesses. In my mind, I was trying to help them, but it caused some to stop coming to the classes in the chapel. My judgments and criticisms prevented them from experiencing the only light they were receiving at the time. Over time, some guys I personally knew transferred to the facility, and they were hustlers.

Every day, I would visit them, engage in conversation, and hang out with them. They offered me some pills. I declined their offer and decided not to visit them again that day. That temptation stuck with me, and the next day I went back over there and took some pills, telling myself that just a few were no problem. It grew worse and became more and more frequent. I was still going to classes in the chapel, but I wasn't talking so much anymore. After some time, my lack of involvement started becoming more noticeable. I even started missing a few classes. I will never forget the morning I was in the yard, high on drugs, walking alone and feeling terrible. I glanced over at my friends, who were gathered in their usual spots, and they were all staring at me and discussing me with each other.

In that very moment, God opened my eyes to see myself over there talking about the others who were struggling. In that moment, I felt horrible. I remember going to bed and crying out to God about it. The following morning, I would resolutely resolve to abstain from drugs for the day. As the day progressed, I would relapse into a "this one last time" mindset and indulge in a high. This pattern of deception and the feeling of powerlessness to overcome it, despite my willingness to quit, tortured me for weeks. I would get high and immediately cry out to God to take it away. I couldn't enjoy it at all, and I couldn't understand why I knew that I wasn't going to enjoy it and still use it. During this time, I felt isolated and couldn't even talk to anybody about it. I felt as though I was imprisoned within a prison.

I used to be facilitating classes in the chapel, discouraging the actions of what I was now living and unable to stop, and it hurt. As time passed, I experienced a renewed sense of strength. A friend of mine started encouraging me, talking about how I was better than that and how to get back up. I continued to use it, albeit less frequently. I resumed my involvement in the chapel, and to God's glory, I regained the strength to triumph. During this time, I became eligible for transfer to an honor camp, and it helped me to clean up my lifestyle. The lesson I learned from judging others is one I will not forget. Luke 6:37–38 says, *"Do not judge, and you will not face judgment. If you refrain from condemning others, they will also refrain from condemning you. Forgive, and you will be forgiven. Give, and you will receive. You will receive a good measure, pressed down, shaken together, and poured over. The measure you employ will determine the outcome for you."*

While I was in error, I couldn't see what God was trying to show me about myself. Once my eyes were opened and I felt others' pain when they saw me talking about them, I began to understand. I was judging, and I was wrong. The yoke of slavery is no joke, and in my sobriety, I somehow forgot that fact. It is extremely difficult to break free from the cycle of addiction and cravings when they are so abundant around you. This lesson was necessary to equip me for the ministry God is calling me into.

Hebrews 12:7-11 says, *"Endure hardship as discipline; God is treating you as his children. For what children are not disciplined by their father? If you are not disciplined—and everyone undergoes discipline—then you are not legitimate, not true sons and daughters at all. Moreover, we have all had human fathers who disciplined us and we respected them for it. How much more should we submit to the Father of spirits and live! They disciplined us for a little while as they thought best; but God disciplines us for our good, in order that we may share in his holiness. No discipline seems pleasant at the time, but painful. Later on, however, it produces a harvest of righteousness and peace for those who have been trained by it."*

I'm certainly not saying that God will tempt you to learn a lesson. In this regard, the Scriptures are clear. James 1:13 says, *"When tempted, no one should say that God is tempting me. Evil cannot tempt God, nor does He tempt anyone."* I am saying that God's mercy and grace are sufficient, so that even in your error, He is able to make it for your good. When He uses your error for your good, He will use it to teach you about your ways, thereby contributing to the building up of the Body of Christ. This is part of the equipping process, as well as the beauty of His grace. The testing of faith produces perseverance. Let perseverance finish its work and equip you. This is also the strength of Jesus, who embodies the image of God in human form and endured every temptation to provide us comfort during our trials. By doing this, Jesus becomes the faithful high priest who stands sinless before God on our behalf. Our Advocate with the Father.

In the Book of Acts, we read about Saul of Tarsus, who was zealous for God. Saul was persecuting the early Christians, but in his mind, he thought he was doing the will of God. Saul was in error in a major way, and Jesus got his attention. Acts 9:1-9 says, *"Meanwhile, Saul was still breathing out murderous threats against the Lord's disciples. He went to the high priest and asked him for letters to the synagogues in Damascus, so that if he found any there who belonged to the Way, whether men or women, he might take them as prisoners to Jerusalem. As he neared Damascus on his journey, suddenly a light from heaven flashed around him. He fell to the ground and heard a voice say to him, "Saul, Saul, why do you persecute me?" "Who are you, Lord?" Saul asked. "I am Jesus, whom you are persecuting," he replied. "Now get up and go into the city, and you will be told what you must do." The men traveling with Saul stood there speechless; they heard the sound but did not see anyone. Saul got up from the ground, but when he opened his eyes he could see nothing. So they led him by the hand into Damascus. For three days he was blind, and did not eat or drink anything."*

Correcting Saul's zealousness for God was necessary. He was in error, not realizing he was persecuting Jesus by attacking His disciples. God was able to transform Saul's zeal from error to proclaiming His name to the nations. In the process, he had to let go of his arrogance. Then Jesus used a man whom Saul was going to persecute to bring healing to Saul's blindness. Saul found himself at the mercy of those whom he sought to persecute. It was a humbling experience for Saul, but necessary for his equipping. We must stop looking at each other's shortcomings and passing judgment on those around us, not knowing what God is doing for their good. God is still in control. Stop looking at your own shortcomings as failure, and seek God for wisdom in the midst of the storm, trusting Him that He is able to calm the storm. Then listen to His voice and learn His truths about you, so that you no longer exchange His truth for the lies of the enemy.

When God called Moses, he could only see his own shortcomings and make his case to God. Exodus 4:10–12 says, *"Moses said to the Lord, Please pardon your servant, Lord. I have never been eloquent, neither in the past nor since you have spoken to your servant. I am slow with my speech and tongue. The Lord said to him, "Who gave humans their mouths?" Who makes them deaf or mute? Who gives them sight, or who makes them blind? Is it not I, the Lord? Now proceed; I will assist you in speaking and provide guidance on what to say."* God's equipping you to fulfill His purpose in your life may seem impossible to you, but God promises to equip the called. Stand by His promises.

Hebrews 13:20-21 says, *"Now may the God of Peace, who through the Blood of the Eternal Covenant brought back from the dead our Lord Jesus, that Great Shepherd of the Sheep, equip you with everything good for doing His will, and may He work in us what is pleasing to Him, through Jesus Christ, to whom be glory forever and ever Amen."* Remember when God called for light to shine out of darkness? Darkness was the platform that the light used to shine from and out of. This is the pattern of a believer's life that the light illuminated.

God calls you to be a light out of darkness. God utilizes the darkness to reveal the light within. Therefore, when you emerge from the darkness, it serves as a platform for your light to shine. Observe the workings of a newly planted seed. A seed planted and covered in soil is in darkness. Its roots grow in darkness, and as it sprouts and grows, its source is the sun's light. God sends rain to hydrate the soil, fostering the growth of the plants. Rainfall, whether excessive or insufficient, can hinder the growth of plants. As the plant grows, it strives to reach its source, which is light. The initial seed must die in order to give birth to the plant, which then produces more seeds.

John 12:24–26 says, *"Very truly I tell you, unless a kernel of wheat falls to the ground and dies, it remains only a single seed. But if it dies, it produces many seeds. Anyone who loves their life will lose it, while anyone who hates their life in this world will keep it for eternal life. Whoever serves me must follow me; and where I am, my servant also will be. My Father will honor the one who serves me."* Jesus said that where I am, my servant will also be. If Jesus lives in you, then you are where Jesus is. Of course, we look at these passages in relation to living in heaven eternally with Jesus. However, Jesus is referring to this passage in the context of a person who is currently living in this world.

The one who loves their life will lose it. The one who hates their life in this world will keep it for eternity. Following Jesus means understanding that His life is alive in you. These Jesus passages are not stories of His achievements, but examples of Him being the living word in you. Jesus' time on earth in the flesh limited His interaction with all of mankind. He chose the twelve disciplines that walked daily with Him. By going to the cross, laying down His life for us, and rising from the dead, He gives us His Spirit to dwell in us as though He were walking with us like He was with the disciples in the flesh. Through His Spirit, it is only possible for Jesus to walk with each of us daily. The Spirit of God living in you is nothing to play with.

Though the enemy tries to battle that spirit with the flesh, we are tempted to indulge the flesh and quench the Holy Spirit that lives in you. Jesus displayed this battle between becoming flesh and being the living word in Gethsemane.

Following Jesus means taking up your cross and living His example as He lives in you through His Spirit. Understanding this truth will open your eyes to the power that lives in you through Jesus. The fact that the Disciples continued to sleep in Gethsemane suggests that they did not comprehend this truth at the time and continue to do so to this day. Acts 1:8 says, *"But you will receive power when the Holy Spirit comes on you, and you will be my witnesses in Jerusalem, in all Judea and Samaria, and to the ends of the earth."*

This receiving of the Holy Spirit is the fulfillment of the promise Jesus made to His disciples, as described in the book of John. John 14:15–21 says, *"If you love me, keep my commands. And I will ask the Father, and he will give you another advocate to help you and be with you forever—the Spirit of truth. The world cannot accept him, because it neither sees him nor knows him. But you know him, for he lives with you and will be in you. I will not leave you as orphans; I will come to you. Before long, the world will not see me anymore, but you will see me. Because I live, you also will live. On that day you will realize that I am in my Father, and you are in me, and I am in you. Whoever has my commands and keeps them is the one who loves me. The one who loves me will be loved by my Father, and I too will love them and show myself to them."*

You are not alone; you are not the enemy's lies that persuade you to think you are not worthy. The enemy does not speak to you through those who manipulate you. It's not them speaking; it's the voice of the one they listen to and are vessels of, the father of lies. You are who Jesus calls you to be. Though we make mistakes, that's not who you are. Get back up and buckle the Belt of Truth around your waist, holding the Breastplate of Righteousness in place. It's the power of the Holy Spirit alive in you. It's only attainable through faith and surrender to Jesus. When Jesus explained these truths to His disciples, they couldn't grasp the significance of His teaching. One disciple named Phillip spoke up and questioned Jesus, but Phillip's perspective and misunderstanding mirror those of many believers today who grapple with this truth.

John 14:6–14 says, *"Jesus answered, I am the way, the truth, and the life." No one comes to the Father except through me. If you really know me, you'll also know my Father. From now on, you do know Him and have seen Him. Phillip said, Lord, show us the Father, and that will be enough for us. Jesus answered, Don't you know me, Phillip, even after I have been among you such a long time? Anyone who has seen me has seen the Father. How can you say, Show us the Father? Don't you think I'm in the Father and the Father in me? In the words I say to you, I do not speak on my own authority. Rather, it is the Father, living in me, who is doing His work. Believe me when I say that I am in the Father and the Father is in me, or at least believe in the evidence of the works themselves. Very truly, I tell you, whoever believes in me will do the works I have been doing, and they will do even greater things than these because I am going to the Father. I will fulfill all your requests in my name, ensuring the glory of the Father through the Son. You may ask me for anything in my name, and I will do it."*

The evidence of the works themselves. Do you have any evidence of Jesus' works in your life? Has He delivered you, provided for you, or kept you from death? Has He performed miracles in your life that you knew had to be God? Phillip's request for Jesus to reveal the Father in the face of overwhelming evidence indicates a lack of faith and unbelief. Jesus is expressing His truth to His disciples in a way that they can do greater works and ask and receive whatever they ask in His name. If your view of Jesus is of His works in the flesh during His time on earth instead of His power at work in you today, then you have the view of those of Jesus' hometown.

Mark 6:1-6 says, *"Jesus left there and went to his home town, accompanied by His disciples. When the Sabbath came, he began to teach in the synagogue, and many who heard him were amazed. Where did this man get these things? What wisdom does this man possess? What are these remarkable miracles that He is performing? Isn't this the carpenter? Isn't this Mary's son and brother to James, Joseph, Judas, and Simon? Aren't his sisters here with us? And they took offense at Him. Jesus told them, A prophet is not without honor except in his own town, among his relatives, and in his own home. He could not do any miracles there, except lay his hands on a few sick people and heal them. He was amazed at their lack of faith."*

The lack of faith and unbelief limited the miraculous power of Jesus. This lack of understanding aids our lack of faith in who Jesus is. We confess that Jesus lives in us. Our body is the living temple of Jesus' Spirit. We are the home of Jesus. The lack of faith in His own home speaks to our lack of faith in who He is. We praise Jesus and glorify His name, yet we doubt He is able to work through us in our own situation. We limit His power in our own lives through our lack of faith and unbelief, not understanding that His Word is alive in us. We make statements such as "I know He can, but..." and "I believe He can, but..." According to Scripture, they were amazed at His teaching. However, they began to focus on the facts about Him, rather than recognizing His true nature. This prevented them from receiving what He was willing to provide. Let us not limit our Lord Jesus because of our lack of faith and unbelief.

He equips us with His Spirit, which lives within us. I used to read these Scriptures with immediate doubt because I had prayed and asked for many things that I had not received. I couldn't understand why Jesus would make this statement: "Ask me anything, and you will receive it." Over time, in my walk with Jesus, I've sought His understanding of this passage, because I know I'm not the only one who feels let down by this promise. I begin to reflect on the numerous instances where I have received what I had prayed for, only to discover over time that it was not what I had anticipated. Consequently, I find myself complaining and pleading with God to transform my request into something else. Is it possible that, in His infinite wisdom, He will close a door you want opened only because of His mercy in knowing what's in store on that path?

Instead of complaining about not receiving everything I ask for, I begin to praise Him for closing a door because I know that He knows what's best for me. Is what's best for you always comforting in the moment? In time, it will make perfect sense, though. In time, looking back, you will praise Jesus for His protection in closing a door that you wanted to open so badly. Knowing this truth gives you the grace of understanding His infinite wisdom. As I began to understand this truth and the fact that I pray for His protection over my life daily, it only made sense that His protection would surpass my desire for what I thought was best. Thank you, Jesus!

9

Persevering And Favor

In John 6:66–70, it states, *"From this time on, many of His disciples turned back and no longer followed Him. You do not want to leave either, do you? Jesus asked the twelve. Simon Peter answered him, Lord, to whom shall we go? You have the words of eternal life. We have come to believe and know that you are God's Holy One. Then Jesus replied, Have I not chosen you, the twelve? Yet one of you is a devil!"* The beginning of knowledge comes when you realize that there really is no place else to turn for truth that leads to eternal life.

Proverbs 1:7 says, *"Fear of the Lord is the beginning of knowledge, but fools despise wisdom and instruction."* Jesus was teaching His disciples, telling them that He was the bread of life. Those in the crowd replied that their ancestors ate manna in the wilderness. Jesus said He is the true bread from heaven that gives life to the world. They found Jesus' teachings difficult to understand. They took His words as though they were to physically eat His flesh and drink His blood. They were unable to grasp that He is the Living Word of God; instead, they looked at Him as the son of Mary and Joseph, not the Son of God. It's the misunderstanding of who Jesus is, and the failure to grasp the power of His resurrection and the fullness of His Spirit alive in you, that can cause a person to lose heart and turn away.

The question from Peter saying, "Lord, to whom shall we go?" is the standing answer that is used to persevere. The world will attempt to draw you back into a life of sin and hopelessness. In moments of trials and feelings of closed doors, the temporary pleasures of sin seem appealing. I have fallen for these deceptions in my life, and I can relate to the ones who may be in this season of their lives. The temporary pleasures are very temporary, and the devil disguises well the consequences of our bad decisions. The beauty of it all is the mercy that God bestows upon us during these seasons. Maybe it was a setback or a failed expectation of what you thought God was going to do for you, but it didn't happen. God is still in control!

The words of Peter ring loud: Lord, to whom shall we go? The parable of the prodigal son illustrates God's grace and mercy to us in these life situations. Luke 15:11-24 says, *"Jesus continued, describing a man who had two sons." The younger one said to his father, 'Father, give me my share of the estate.' He then divided his property between them. Shortly afterward, the younger son gathered all his belongings, embarked on a journey to a far-off country, and squandered his wealth on extravagant lifestyles. Once he had exhausted all his resources, a severe famine struck the entire country, leaving him in dire need. So he went and hired himself out to a citizen of that country, who sent him to his fields to feed pigs. He longed to fill his stomach with the pods that the pigs were eating, but no one gave him anything. When he regained consciousness, he exclaimed, "How many of my father's hired servants have enough food to spare, and here I am starving to death?" I will set out and go back to my father, saying to him, Father, I have sinned against Heaven and against you. I no longer deserve the title of your son; treat me as one of your hired servants. He stood up and made his way towards his father. But while he was still a long way off, his father saw him and was filled with compassion for him. He ran to his son, threw his arms around him, and kissed him. Father, I have sinned against Heaven and against you; I am no longer worthy to call myself your son. But the father said to his servants, Quick! Bring the best robe and put it on him. He placed a ring on his finger and sandals on his feet. Bring the fattened calf and kill it. Let's have a feast and celebrate. This son of mine was once dead, but now he has returned to life; he was once lost, but now he has found his way back. So they began to celebrate."*

Genesis 37:5-8 says, *"Joseph had a dream, and when he told it to his brothers, they hated him all the more. He told them, 'Listen to this dream I had: We were binding sheaves of grain out in the field when suddenly my sheaf rose and stood upright, while your sheaves gathered around mine and bowed down to it.' His brothers said to him, 'Do you intend to reign over us? Will you actually rule us?' Because of his dream and words, they hated him more."* This created a dangerous situation for Joseph because his brothers were plotting to kill him at the time.

One day, while Joseph's brothers were out in the field grazing their flocks, Jacob sent Joseph to go and check on his brothers. When Joseph found his brothers, they saw him coming in the distance. In Genesis 37:19-20, they said to each other, *"Here comes that dreamer!" Come now. Let's kill him, throw him into one of these cisterns, and say that a ferocious animal devoured him. Then we'll see what comes of his dreams."* The hatred that Joseph's brothers had against him would have cost Joseph his life, but God was with him. In this very situation, God's favor doesn't appear to be as we have come to know it. The favor of God is that in order for Joseph's dream to come true, some things had to happen in Joseph's life, and his brother's betrayal had to take place. Although they planned to kill Joseph, they ultimately sold him as a slave to the Ishmaelites, who were Midianite merchants who took Joseph to Egypt.

Genesis 39:1–5 says, *"Now Joseph had been taken down to Egypt. Potiphar, an Egyptian who was one of Pharaoh's officials, the captain of the guard, bought him from the Ishmaelites who had taken him there. The Lord was with Joseph so that he prospered, and he lived in the house of his Egyptian master. When his master saw that the Lord was with him and that the Lord gave him success in everything he did, Joseph found favor in his eyes and became his attendant. Potiphar put him in charge of his household, and he entrusted to his care everything he owned. From the time he put him in charge of his household and of all that he owned, the Lord blessed the household of the Egyptian because of Joseph. The blessing of the Lord was on everything Potiphar had, both in the house and in the field."*

According to the Bible, the Lord was with Joseph so that he could prosper. The fact that his brothers threw him into a cistern and ultimately sold him as a slave does not appear to indicate that the Lord was with him. During difficult times in our lives, it can seem as though the Lord is not by our side. I find myself questioning God during these times. Lord, why is this happening? Lord, why are you allowing this to take place? In the midst of these trials and storms, it doesn't feel like I'm blessed and highly favored. I've had to expand my understanding of what true favor is. God's favor is aligning circumstances that ultimately turn out for your benefit. This alignment process can bring tough times and uncomfortable circumstances that we must persevere through to see the positioning of what God is doing in our lives.

People may betray you; they may walk out of your life. You might face rejection or denial of what you genuinely desire. These times will test your faith. The moment may make no sense and make you feel rejected by God. You can lean on your own understanding through these times and try to force things to go the way you want, which leads to frustration and despair. Or you can grow in your trust in the Almighty God and believe that if He allowed this to happen, then it was for a reason, and I'm going to trust Him. If people leave your life, trust them and believe that their actions have no bearing on where God is leading you. Trust in the fact that God is in control. During these trying times, speak life into your future and circumstances instead of listening to the lies of the enemy that make you feel less than how God sees you.

Joseph's brothers openly spoke against his dreams. The dreams of Joseph incited jealousy and anger in their hearts. Joseph's dreams came to life due to the Lord's presence. If the Lord is repositioning your surroundings and circumstances, trust that He is in control. The process can hurt your feelings and cause difficult circumstances, but persevere, knowing God has your back. Stand by His promises and speak the word that is alive in you. James 1:2-4 says, *"Consider it pure joy, my brothers and sisters, whenever you face trials of many types, because you know that the testing of your faith produces perseverance. Let perseverance finish its work so that you may be mature and complete, not lacking anything."*

How is it possible to consider it pure joy while going through trials of many kinds? The repositioning process has begun, and God's favor is at work. You come to this understanding as you let perseverance finish its work in your life. To become mature and complete, you must have complete confidence in His ability to guide your life for your benefit. Shift your attention from the circumstances to the visible. Instead, fix your eyes on the unseen by Faith. 2 Corinthians 4:17–18 says, *"For our light and momentary troubles are achieving for us an eternal glory that far outweighs them all. So we fix our eyes not on what is seen, but on what is unseen, since what is seen is temporary, but what is unseen is eternal."*

We gain confidence in the face of many trials by knowing that God's hand is working some things in our favor. This brings joy to a situation that would normally cause you sorrow and unbelief. Let perseverance finish its work in you. As you persevere, you will receive a crown of life. James 1:12 *"Blessed is the one who perseveres under trial because, having stood the test, that person will receive the crown of life that the Lord has promised to those who love Him."* Joseph had to persevere through difficult-to-overcome situations up to this point. It doesn't get any easier at this point in his life, either. He had to rearrange more aspects of his life to realize his dreams. The Bible describes Joseph as well-built and handsome.

Joseph was Potiphar's servant, and the Lord blessed everything Potiphar owned because of him. Potiphar's wife noticed Joseph and told him to come to bed with her. Joseph refused time and again. Genesis 39:9-21 *"No one is greater in this house than I am. My master has withheld nothing from me except you, because you are his wife. How then could I do such a wicked thing and sin against God?" And though she spoke to Joseph day after day, he refused to go to bed with her or even be with her. One day he went into the house to attend to his duties, and none of the household servants was inside. She caught him by his cloak and said, "Come to bed with me!" But he left his cloak in her hand and ran out of the house. When she saw that he had left his cloak in her hand and had run out of the house, she called her household servants. "Look," she said to them, "this Hebrew has been brought to us to make sport of us! He came in here to sleep with me, but I screamed. When he heard me scream for help, he left his cloak beside me and ran out of the house." She kept his cloak beside her until his master came home. Then she told him this story: "That Hebrew slave you brought us came to me to make sport of me. But as soon as I screamed for help, he left his cloak beside me and ran out of the house." When his master heard the story his wife told him, saying, "This is how your slave treated me," he burned with anger. Joseph's master took him and put him in prison, the place where the king's prisoners were confined. But while Joseph was there in the prison, the Lord was with him; he showed him kindness and granted him favor in the eyes of the prison warden."*

The kindness and favor of the Lord did not prevent Joseph from a fiery trial; they enabled him to persevere through it. Joseph could have grown bitter and given up on life. The odds were definitely against him. Despite their desire to kill him, Joseph's brothers hated him and sold him as a slave to foreigners. The fact was that Joseph was imprisoned for an attempted rape he did not commit. It doesn't appear that the Lord was with him, nor that the Lord's favor was upon him. Year after year, he remained in prison with no prospect of release. By all accounts, this looks like a man condemned by God Himself.

His life was a history of betrayals and terrible luck. If God was with him, why didn't he protect him? If God was favoring Joseph, why did all these things happen to him? Betrayed by his own brothers and sold to foreigners as a teenager, Joseph endured heartbreak. He experienced the agony of standing by his moral convictions and refusing to have sex with his master's wife, only to face condemnation from the master as if he had tried to rape her. Joseph reasoned to seriously doubt life itself. Joseph had reason to doubt that God was with him. It can be challenging to persevere if you concentrate on the details of your situation rather than having faith in the One who is ultimately in control. Rather than seeing himself imprisoned under false pretenses, pitying himself with doubt and fear, and dreading life itself, Joseph chose to persevere. Joseph began to see that even in this place, he was as close to the king of Egypt as he'd ever been. Joseph knew from his dreams that he was to be a ruler.

If prison brought him into a position to be close to someone who was a ruler, then his dream still had hope. Although the facts seem to imply that God's favor would keep a man from prison, The truth is, that God's favor can also save a man from prison. Genesis 39:22-23 says, *"So the warden put Joseph in charge of all those held in the prison, and he was made responsible for all that was done there. The warden paid no attention to anything under Joseph's care, because the Lord was with Joseph and gave him success in whatever he did."*

Perseverance brought favor and success in whatever Joseph did. Despite his circumstances, Joseph utilized the gift of dream interpretation he received from the Lord. Despite the circumstances of his current situation, Joseph persevered. At the appointed time, the opportunity presented itself, and through his gift, his dreams would come true. Genesis 40:1-3 says, *"Some time later, the cupbearer and the baker of the king of Egypt offended their master, the king of Egypt. Pharaoh was angry with his two officials, the chief cupbearer and the chief baker, and put them in custody in the house of the captain of the guard, in the same prison where Joseph was confined."*

The cupbearer and the baker were in prison with Joseph after some time, and both had a dream on the same night. Joseph, seeing them, asked why they were so sad. They explained their dreams to Joseph, and he interpreted them. Joseph interpreted the cup bearer's dream as his return to the service of Pharaoh. Upon hearing the favorable interpretation of the cup-bearer's dream, the baker also sought his own interpretation. The baker's dream, however, was of his execution. While Joseph interpreted the cup-bearer's dream of his restoration, Joseph asked him to remember him and mention him to Pharaoh so he could be released from prison. Three days later, a ceremony took place, leading to the execution of the baker and the restoration of the cupbearer. At the time, however, the cup-bearer did not mention Joseph to Pharaoh.

It wasn't until two more years had passed that Pharaoh had a dream and summoned all of Egypt's magicians and wise men, who were unable to interpret it. An important lesson in this parable is the value of the son, not the squandering of his share. The father was overjoyed that his son had come back home. The hardships the son endured while feeding the pigs made him yearn for his return home. Over time, things that initially entice us to regress will eventually lose their allure. Separating from God is not a pleasant feeling. The faithfulness and love of our God in these times is what draws a person to repent. It takes this type of experience for the worldly pleasures that seek to gratify the flesh to lose their grip. I had to slip backwards a few times to realize that life was not for me.

The faithfulness and loving kindness of God, who was willing to meet me in my mess and unfaithfulness, are what it took for me to finally say, Lord, to whom shall we go? You have the words for eternal life. We have come to believe and know that you are God's Holy One. The favor of God in your life can appear to be quite the opposite. The favor of God on the son's life seemed at the time of a severe famine to be a curse or chastening. However, it is the love of God that draws a person to repent. The favor of God in your life can take you through some rough patches in order to fulfill a higher purpose for your life. At the moment, it can feel and appear as if God has forsaken you or turned His back on you. But in time, you will see the hand of God over your life.

This is true for Joseph's life and his experiences. We can learn a lot about God's favor from the story of Joseph in Genesis. Joseph was the youngest son of Jacob, and his father favored him. Joseph's father's favoritism led to his brothers' despising of him. When he was 17 years old, Joseph told his brothers about a dream that he had. It was then that the cupbearer remembered Joseph and mentioned him to Pharaoh. Pharaoh promptly summoned Joseph from the dungeon. When he had shaved and changed his clothes, he came before Pharaoh. Pharaoh said to Joseph, 'I had a dream, and no one can interpret it. However, I've heard that you have the ability to interpret dreams. Joseph replied to Pharaoh, "I cannot do it, but God will give Pharaoh the answer he desires."

Joseph's confidence in this moment is admirable. He quickly denied himself in the moment and gave honor to God, who would provide the answer. Joseph's perseverance and reverence for the Lord were on display. All that Joseph has endured in his life to this point and his complete reliance on the Lord present a beautiful picture we should strive to emulate. Joseph demonstrated a remarkable level of patience and humility. Pharaoh shared his dreams with Joseph, and not only did Joseph interpret them, but God also bestowed upon Joseph wisdom and guidance, which he then communicated to Pharaoh, ensuring Egypt's survival during the famine. The interpretation of Pharaoh's dreams revealed seven years of great abundance, followed by seven years of famine. Joseph suggested to Pharaoh that he find a wise and discerning man and put him in charge of Egypt's land. Who will set aside a fifth of the harvest during the seven years of abundance to prevent the famine from ruining them?

Genesis 41:37–43 states, *"The plan seemed good to Pharaoh and to all his officials. So Pharaoh asked them, "Can we find anyone like this man, one in whom is the spirit of God?" Then Pharaoh said to Joseph, "Since God has made all this known to you, there is no one so discerning and wise as you. You shall be in charge of my palace, and all my people are to submit to your orders. Only with respect to the throne will I be greater than you." So Pharaoh said to Joseph, "I hereby put you in charge of the whole land of Egypt." Then Pharaoh took his signet ring from his finger and put it on Joseph's finger. He dressed him in robes of fine linen and put a gold chain around his neck. He had him ride in a chariot as his second-in-command, and people shouted before him, "Make way!" Thus he put him in charge of the whole land of Egypt."*

Joseph endured ridicule, hatred, betrayal, and imprisonment throughout his life, yet God continued to favor him. It's a refreshing example for those of us who have to endure such hardships in this life. Whether by our own bad decisions, fate, and circumstances, or a combination of all, there remains a promise from the Lord that He is with us, and through faith in Jesus, we have His Spirit in us. Where the Spirit of the Lord is, there is freedom and liberty. Joseph was able to secure the land and keep food in reserve during the famine. His brothers eventually arrived in Egypt to buy food from Joseph. Although Joseph kept his identity from his brothers for a time, he eventually revealed his identity to them. In doing so, Joseph made a powerful proclamation that resonates with us today.

When Joseph lost control in front of all his attendants, he cried out, "Have everyone leave my presence!" No one was with Joseph when he told his brothers. And he wept so loudly that the Egyptians heard him, and Pharaoh's household heard about it. Joseph declared to his brothers, I am Joseph! Is my father still living? However, his brothers were unable to answer him because they were terrified of his presence. Then Joseph said to his brothers, Come close to me. When they had done so, he said, I am your brother Joseph, the one you sold into Egypt! Now, do not be distressed or angry with yourselves for selling me here, for God sent me ahead of you to save lives. For two years now, there has been famine in the land, and for the next five years, there will be no plowing or reaping.

But God sent me ahead of you to preserve for you a remnant on earth and to save your lives through a great deliverance. So then it was not you, but God, who sent me here. He made me father to Pharaoh, lord of his entire household and ruler of all of Egypt. "What was meant for evil, God used for good. This is the pattern of light emerging from darkness. This is perseverance and favor. No matter what you have done, it is not out of God's reach. He is in control, so give him control of your situation. The call to persevere is a call to each one of us. Let perseverance finish its work in you. Know the beautiful promises of God spoken over you as His own and trust Him with His favor, knowing that in this life you will have troubles, but Jesus overcame the world.

John 16:33 says, *"I have told you these things so that you may have peace in me." You will encounter difficulties in this world. But take heart! I have overcome the world."* Thank you, Jesus, for your love for us. Let us not take Your words in vain, but use Your words as our life in You. Teach us with Your Spirit, and give us strength to persevere as we look to You to lead us and guide us through this life. Fill us with Your Spirit and Power, and give us a vision of our purpose in You. We trust in you, Lord. In Jesus name, Amen. Show us the way.

10

No FEAR

2 Timothy 1:7 states, "For *God did not give us a spirit of fear, but of power, love, and self-control.*" The Word of God says 365 times throughout the Scriptures to fear not. This is relative to the enemy's attempt every day to inflict fearful thoughts into our minds pertaining to our lives. Being in a state of fear is contrary to your standing as a child of God. We may say that we don't struggle with fear like that, not realizing that the roots of a lot of the things we struggle with are fearful. Fear is the root of insecurity and thoughts of unworthiness. Fear is the root of worrying about what others are thinking about you. Fear is the root of doubting what God has shown you to do.

I struggle to this day with thoughts and feelings of insecurity. Whether it's dealing with family, friends, loved ones, relationships, or being in ministry, my insecurities have surfaced. The enemy has attacked my feelings of worthiness time and again. In doing so, I've come to grow in realizing that I've been so quick to accuse others of things, yet it was only my insecurities of feeling unworthy to receive in the first place. By doing this, I have allowed the enemy to rob me and keep me in a place of isolation where I'm tormented in my mind with thoughts of not being good enough. This is the attribute of the thief who comes to steal, kill, and destroy. Time and again, as I look back over my life, I have allowed the enemy to steal, kill, and destroy. Feelings of insecurity can foster a negative outlook, which in turn attracts the negativity I continue to express about myself and my circumstances. Yet I've been ignorant of the Word of God concerning myself and buying into the lies of the enemy all this time.

John 10:10 says, "The *thief comes only to steal, kill, and destroy; I have come that they may have life and have it to the full.*" The spirit of suspicion is not to be confused with the spirit of discernment. In dealing with people, whether in business deals, relationships, or friendships, I realized that my fear of being done wrong will drive my thoughts to seek accusation to confirm the suspicion in my mind that will drive away something beneficial to me. In my mind, my suspicion is justified, yet in time I come to see that I was dead wrong all along. How could this be? What is driving my thoughts this way? The simple answer is fear, but the complexity of fear runs in several different directions. Feeling unworthy will prohibit your acceptance of love and affection.

Someone telling you they love you will begin to irritate you. Then the same person, not telling you they love you, will feed your suspicion you had all along and bring an accusation against them. The root of it all is fear. A great opportunity that presents itself to you will bring doubt to its authenticity. The fear of rejection and failure will then drive you away from something intended to benefit you. Then, we doubt God's ability to fulfill our needs, unaware that He has placed them before us, allowing the thief to steal, kill, and destroy them. He does it by creating fear in your mind concerning the things God has for you. Failure to grow spiritually and understand the Words of God spoken over and alive in you will hinder you and make you susceptible to the traps of the enemy.

Jesus said, I have come so that they may have life and have it to the full. This is in direct response to the warning about the thief who comes to steal, kill, and destroy. Understanding these truths shines a light on how to apply the words of Jesus spoken in Luke. Luke 6:27-36 says, *"But to you who are listening I say: Love your enemies, do good to those who hate you, bless those who curse you, pray for those who mistreat you. If someone slaps you on one cheek, turn to them the other also. If someone takes your coat, do not withhold your shirt from them. Give to everyone who asks you, and if anyone takes what belongs to you, do not demand it back. Do to others as you would have them do to you." If you love those who love you, what credit is that to you? Even sinners love those who love them. And if you do good to those who are good to you, what credit is that to you? Even sinners do that. And if you lend to those from whom you expect repayment, what credit is that to you? Even sinners lend to sinners, expecting to be repaid in full. But love your enemies, do good to them, and lend to them without expecting to get anything back. Then your reward will be great, and you will be children of the Most High, because he is kind to the ungrateful and wicked. Be merciful, just as your Father is merciful."*

Living out these truths of Jesus is impossible while living in a state of fear and only possible if you completely trust Him. It's hard not to allow fearful thoughts of factual loss that, in our minds, place us in jeopardy of our finances and well-being. However, standing on these truths places you in a position for the Father to reward you. It takes faith and trust, the absence of fear, and leaning on Him who will provide. Taking the posture of accusation against one another places us in the position of our adversary, as described in Revelations 12:10: *"Then I heard a loud voice in Heaven say: Now have come the salvation and the power and the kingdom of our God, and the authority of His Messiah. For the accuser of our brothers and sisters, who accuses them before our God day and night, has been hurled down."*

I'm beginning to understand that the accusations I make, driven by fear, against others don't stem from my ability to discern but rather, they align with the father of lies and serve his agenda. This truth changed my perspective and gave me freedom in major ways in my life. I'm not saying that people won't do you wrong. I'm not saying that the evil desires of others won't try you. Because He who lives in you is greater than He in the world, fear shouldn't keep you from good.

Discernment is distinguishing between the spirits, knowing good from evil. We read about the spiritual gifts in 1 Corinthians. 1 Corinthians 12:10 says, *"To another miraculous powers, to another prophecy, to another distinguishing between spirits, to another speaking in different kinds of tongues, and to still another the interpretation of tongues."* The enemy uses a generalized form of discernment called the spirit of suspicion, which brings accusations without being able to tell good from evil, to sow discord by instilling fear in people about what they are suspicious of. Having an understanding of this truth will enable you to be free of fear, knowing that God is in control and will bring to light the deeds of darkness. This level of solid food takes constant use to develop.

Hebrews 5:13-14 tells us that, "Anyone *who lives on milk, being still an infant, is not acquainted with the teaching about righteousness. But solid food is for the mature, who by constant use have trained themselves to distinguish good from evil."* Examples of great men in the Scriptures who were susceptible to fear even after experiencing great victories from God are to encourage us and teach us that God is faithful even in the face of our fears. A prophet named Elijah, a mighty man of God, experienced and performed miracles from God in mighty ways. During the time that Ahab was King of Israel, Ahab had abandoned the Lord's commands and followed the Baals.

1 Kings 16:30-33 says, *"Ahab son of Omri did more evil in the eyes of the Lord than any of those before him. He not only considered it trivial to commit the sins of*

Jeroboam son of Nebat, but he also married Jezebel daughter of Ethbaal king of the Sidonians, and began to serve Baal and worship him. He set up an altar for Baal in the temple of Baal that he built in Samaria. Ahab also made an Asherah pole and did more to arouse the anger of the Lord, the God of Israel, than did all the kings of Israel before him." Baal was a pagan god that represented fertility and rain. Ahab turned from the Lord to serve a pagan god and aroused the anger of the Lord. God sends Elijah to proclaim a drought in the land to show the people that Baal is not the source of rain.

1 Kings 17:1 says, *"Now Elijah, the Tishbite from Tishbe in Gilead, said to Ahab, As the Lord the God of Israel lives, whom I serve, there will be neither dew nor rain in the next few years except at my word."* As the drought persisted over the next few years, Ahab had sent word to bring Elijah to him. Over the course of this time, Elijah was hidden by the Lord. When the appointed time came, the Lord sent Elijah to Ahab, who blamed Elijah for the drought. 1 Kings 18:16-19 says, *"So Obadiah went to meet Ahab and told him, and Ahab went to meet Elijah. When he saw Elijah, he said to him, is that you, you troubler of Israel? I have not made trouble for Israel, Elijah replied. But you and your fathers family have. You have abandoned the Lord's commands and have followed the Baals. Now summon the people from all over Israel to meet me on Mount Carmel. And bring the four hundred and fifty prophets of Baal and the four hundred prophets of Asherah, who eat at Jezebel's table."*

Elijah had Ahab bring the prophets of Baal to Mount Carmel. Then he instructed them to get two bulls. Elijah had the prophets of Baal slaughter one of the bulls and place it on an altar of wood. He then did the same with the other. Elijah then instructed them to call on their god, and Elijah would call on the Lord, and whoever answers by fire, He is God. The prophets of Baal went first and began to call on Baal. After a while of no answer, Elijah began to taunt the prophets of Baal.

1 Kings 18:26-29 says, *"So they took the bull given them and prepared it. Then they called on the name of Baal from morning till noon. 'Baal answer us!' they shouted. But there was no response, no one answered. And they danced around the altar they had made. At noon Elijah began to taunt them. 'Shout louder!' he said. ' Surely he is a god! Perhaps he is in deep thought, or busy, or traveling. Maybe he is sleeping and must be awakened.' So they shouted louder and slashed themselves with swords and spears, as was their custom, until their blood flowed. Midday passed, and they continued their frantic prophesying until the time for the evening sacrifice. But there was no response, no one answered, no one paid attention."*

Elijah taunting hundreds of the prophets of Baal and standing alone physically doing so is obvious that he does not fear. Elijah is confident that the Lord is with him and will protect him in this moment. As they cut themselves with swords and spears and caused their own blood to flow, Elijah taunts them. He was not afraid of their violence against him. He was completely trusting in the Lord to be with him, and it was obvious that the Lord was with Elijah. At this point, Elijah was so confident he had them dig trenches around the altar and pour water over the bull and the altar, soaking it wet with water.

1 Kings 18:36-39 says, *"At the time of sacrifice, the prophet Elijah stepped forward and prayed, "Lord, the God of Abraham, Isaac, and Israel, let it be known today that you are God in Israel and that I am your servant and have done all these things at your command. Answer me, Lord, answer me, so these people will know that you, Lord, are God and that you are turning their hearts back again." Then the fire of the Lord fell and burned up the sacrifice, the wood, the stones and the soil, and also licked up the water in the trench. When all the people saw this, they fell prostrate and cried, "The Lord—he is God! The Lord—he is God!"* After this took place, Elijah seized the prophets of Baal and had them slaughtered. Then Elijah told Ahab to go eat and drink because there is the sound of heavy rain. Elijah trusted in the Lord and was full of strength in this moment. He had witnessed the hand of God working through him in mighty ways. He had his

servant go and look for a sign of rain, and on the seventh time, the servant reported a cloud rising out of the sea the size of a man's hand. Upon hearing this, Elijah sent word to Ahab to hitch up his chariot before the rain stops him. The sky grew black, the wind blew harder, and a heavy rain started falling.

Elijah was so full of the Spirit and Power of God that he outran Ahab, who was riding his chariot to the city of Jezreel. The faith and absence of fear in Elijah are remarkable. The Lord sent ravens to feed Elijah after he spoke about the impending drought and during his hiding. The ravens brought him bread and meat every day to eat. Elijah experienced the provision of the Lord in miraculous ways. The widow and her son welcomed Elijah into their home. While there, the widow told Elijah that she only had a handful of flour and a little oil left. She said that she was going to make one last meal for herself and her son and die. The effects of the drought were affecting everyone. Elijah instructed her to make a loaf of bread, promising that the flour she had and the oil in the jar would not run out until the Lord sent rain on the land.

Elijah is witnessing the provision of the Lord yet again. After some time, the widow's son fell ill and eventually passed away. Elijah took the boy to the upstairs room and laid him on the bed. Elijah cried out to the Lord on behalf of the widow and her son, stretching himself over the boy three times and pleading for the return of his life. The Lord heard Elijah's prayer, and the boy's life returned to him. Elijah returned the boy to his mother, saying, "Look, your son is alive." She replied, "Now I know that you are a man of God and that the Word of the Lord from your mouth is the truth."

All of these and more miraculous things Elijah witnessed before the fire of the Lord consumed the altar, and he slaughtered the prophets of Baal. Then the rain came and ended the drought according to the Word of the Lord spoken through Elijah. Elijah felt the power of the Lord so strongly that nothing could slow him down. 1 Kings 19:1-4 says, *"Now Ahab told Jezebel everything Elijah had done and how he had killed all the prophets with the sword. So Jezebel sent a messenger to Elijah to say, may the gods deal with me, be it ever so severely, if by this time tomorrow I do not make your life like that of one of them. Elijah was afraid and ran for his life. When he came to Beersheba in Judah, he left his servant there, while he himself went a days journey into the wilderness. He came to a broom bush, sat down under it and prayed that he might die. ' I have had enough Lord,' he said. 'Take my life I am no better than my ancestors."*

Here is Elijah, a mighty man of God, who has witnessed the power of God at work in him and through him. He just witnessed the Fire of God come down and consume the sacrifice and bring rain, ending the drought. The messenger of evil bringing threats against us can cause us to quickly forget the power of God we have witnessed in our own lives. Like Elijah, we can become afraid in the midst of the report from the messenger and run for our lives. I'm thankful for examples like this in the Scriptures. The Scriptures expose the mighty men of God in their moments of weakness, mirroring my own moments of weakness. It's encouraging to know that the miracles that God has done through people who are subject to the same faults as ourselves, He can do through us as well. We have the examples to gain insight and learn from the Word of God how to handle situations that arise in our lives.

When the messenger comes and plants a bad report in our minds, what do we do? We can believe the report and go on a day's journey into the wilderness like Elijah. There he prayed to die. When we believe a bad report, we go into the wilderness. The wilderness is a place where hopelessness breeds temptations and the desire to give up on life itself. The devil tempted Jesus in the wilderness. The wilderness is that place of isolation where the enemy can do his work. Notice Elijah left his servant and continued on a day's journey into the wilderness. He was in turmoil and anguish to the point of praying not for protection but to die. This is a dangerous place, directly under the control of the devil. Suicidal thoughts are considered common in the wilderness. The devil wants nothing more than to drag you into the wilderness and convince you that life is not worth living anymore.

We can read this example of Elijah and pass judgment on his weakness and think, How could he be so weak with the obvious power of God in him? Or we can see the example of Elijah as we observe ourselves and see that we too fall for the lies of the messenger in the face of the Power of God that dwells in us. Elijah was a firsthand witness of the provisions of God. The ravens fed him as God commanded. Everything in creation is subjected to His authority—everything. Elijah witnessed the dead brought back to life. We are witnesses of our dead past brought back to a new life only by the power of Jesus. Yet a messenger can deliver fearful threats that control our minds so much that we let them fester in our thoughts as we wander into the wilderness.

This is a threat from Jezebel, who is upset that Elijah slaughtered the prophets of Baal with the sword. It seems so senseless to think that she could follow through with this threat knowing the power of God that is on Elijah. Yet in these weak moments we will fall for the most ridiculous threats that, when we look back over our lives, not only were they empty threats, but we will question how we fell for them in the first place. Thankfully, God is faithful to us; even in our mess, He will send His angels to strengthen us. 1 Kings 19:5-8 says, *"Then he lay down under the bush and fell asleep. All at once, an angel touched him and said, 'Get up and eat'. He looked around, and there by his head was some bread baked over hot coals and a jar of water. He ate and drank and then laid down again. The Angel of the Lord came back a second time and touched him and said, 'Get up and eat, for the journey is too much for you.' So he got up and ate and drank. Strengthened by that food, he traveled forty days and forty nights until he reached Horeb, the Mountain of God."*

Jesus is the Bread of Life. The Bread by which we gain our strength. The Living Word of God. Jesus assures us that the water He provides will transform into a spring within us, leading to eternal life. How many times in our weakness and in the wilderness has a spoken word been given to you? How many times in these situations does an encouraging word from the Bread of Life come to you, and you feel the Spirit of God drawing you? It may have to come at you again and again. Elijah eating the bread and going back to sleep speaks to us that we may need it over and over again, but God is faithful. The strengthening He gave Elijah is available to us today.

In these moments of our lives, if we will submit to Him, He will strengthen us and open our eyes to His will. 1 Kings 19:9–13 says, *"There he went into a cave and spent the night. And the Word of the Lord came to him: 'What are you doing here Elijah?' He replied, 'I have been zealous for the Lord God Almighty. The Israelites have rejected Your Covenant, torn down Your Altars, and put Your Prophets to death with the sword. I am the only one left and they are trying to kill me too'. The Lord said, 'Go out and stand on the mountain in the presence of the Lord, for the Lord is about to pass by'. Then a great and powerful wind tore the mountains apart and shattered the rocks before the Lord, but the Lord was not in the wind. After the wind there was an earthquake, but the Lord was not in the earthquake. After the earthquake, came a fire, but the Lord was not in the fire. And after the fire came a gentle whisper. When Elijah heard it, he pulled his cloak over his face and went out and stood at the mouth of the cave. Then a voice said to him, What are you doing here Elijah?"*

Elijah begins to communicate his thoughts and feelings to the Lord. Elijah brings his concerns and fears before God. God responds by having Elijah go stand on the mountain in the presence of the Lord. This is a picture of Elijah revealing his fears to the Lord. The Lord sent the mighty wind, but the Lord was not in the wind. This illustrates to Elijah that the Lord has control over the wind. Then the earthquake and fire show Elijah that the Lord controls the earthquake and fire but is not in the earthquake and fire. Finally, a gentle whisper shows Elijah that the Lord is in him and assures him of His voice above the voices of the wind, earthquake, and fire. God is in control! In these moments of our lives, as we pour out our fears and concerns to Him, He will assure us of His voice above the voices of our circumstances.

The issue arises when I conceal my fears, allowing them to consume me and instill doubt as I journey through the wilderness. Instead of voicing my fears and concerns to God and truly trusting in Him, I would create a negative outlook and speak the negative thoughts that bring the destructive winds, earthquakes, and fire into my life. Then continue to question God as to why these things are happening in my life. The gentle whisper takes Faith to hear. The bread and water that bring strength take a relationship with Jesus. You can achieve this by studying His Words, meditating on Him, seeking Him as the Good Shepherd of your life, and obeying Him as He teaches you how to apply His Truth to your life. It's the relationship with Jesus and the daily walk with Him.

Just like He did for Elijah, He will do for you. He put Elijah back on assignment. 1 Kings 19:15-18 says, *"The Lord said to him, 'Go back the way you came, and go to the Desert of Damascus. When you get there, anoint Hazael king over Aram. Also anoint Jehu son of Nimshi king over Israel, and anoint Elisha son of Shaphat from Abel Meholah to succeed you as Prophet. Jehu will put to death any who escape the sword of Hazael, and Elisha will put to death any who escape the sword of Jehu. Yet I reserve seven thousand in Israel all whose knees have not bowed down to Baal and whose mouths have not kissed him."* Expect God, when He draws you out of the wilderness and strengthens you, to place you back on assignment for Him. In doing so, the concerns of what you feared diminish and are no longer concerns at all. Learn from these experiences as you walk with Him and live fearlessly. In these moments of our lives, if we will submit to Him, He will strengthen us and open our eyes to His will.

Expect God, when He draws you out of the wilderness and strengthens you, to place you back on assignment for Him. In doing so, the concerns of what you feared diminish and are no longer concerns at all. Grow from these experiences in Him as you walk with Him and, in doing so, live life with no fear.

11

The Wicked Flesh

Romans 7:24-25 states, *"What a wretched man I am! Who will save me from this body that is destined for death? Thank you God for delivering me through Jesus Christ, our Lord! So then, I myself, in my mind, am a slave to God's law, but in my sinful nature, I am a slave to the law of sin."* This is the wonderful dilemma we all face. People often discuss this subject behind the pulpit, but they don't preach it with conviction because it requires the speaker to reveal themselves. Most times, a person is quick to cover up their struggles with their sinful nature, but truthfully, it's a sentence we are all serving. It's common for us to shield ourselves when discussing this subject, yet true freedom stems from being transparent and truthful with ourselves, God, and those closest to us. Small group meetings allow people to bond, confess, and pray for healing.

James 5:16-20 tells us, *"Therefore, confess your sins to each other and pray for each other so that you may be healed. The prayer of a righteous person is powerful and effective. Elijah was a human being, just like us. He prayed earnestly that it would not rain, and it did not rain on the land for three and a half years. Again he prayed, and the heavens gave rain, and the earth produced its crops. My brothers and sisters, if one of you should wander from the truth and someone should bring that person back, remember this: Whoever turns a sinner from the error of their way will save them from death and cover a multitude of sins."* I thought Jesus paid the sin debt for us. He did, and we find salvation through grace. Ephesians 2:8-10 says, *"For grace has saved you through faith, not from yourselves; it is the gift of God, not by works, so no one can boast." For we are God's handiwork, created in Christ Jesus to do beneficial works, which God prepared in advance for us to do."*

It seems confusing and doesn't make sense that Jesus came to this earth, the Word made flesh, laid down His life for us while we were yet sinners, and paid the debt of sin for us. However, our inherent sinful nature continues to challenge us. Jesus sacrificed Himself on the cross for the world, allowing grace to save us through faith in Him. Grace receives what you do not deserve. Mercy is not receiving what you deserve. Understanding the meaning of grace and mercy helps us comprehend God's purposes. We praise Him for His grace and mercy toward us.

Faith saves us by allowing us to receive what we do not deserve. It's only possible if you believe in Jesus and His finished work on the cross. You must believe that He rose from the grave and now resides within you. Defending your faith, which serves as the foundation for receiving grace, is crucial to comprehending why we continue to struggle with our sinful nature despite the payment of our sin debt. Faith is to be tested. If you claim grace yet have no faith, you are deceived. His grace only saves you through faith. Understanding faith and its expression is crucial.

The Scripture says it's not based on one's efforts, so no one can credit it. This is true; Jesus made the way for us. It's not because of our actions; it's because of our faith. However, the Scripture also says that we are God's handiwork, created in Christ Jesus to do beneficial works, which God prepared in advance for us to do. The opportunity to express our faith, through which we receive grace and salvation, is the beneficial work that God has prepared for us to do. The enemy attacks these beneficial works, expressions of our faith, by appealing to our fleshly desires and sinful nature. The enemy uses a deceptive strategy to lure you into a life of sin that contradicts the expression of faith and persuades you that grace covers it, making it acceptable. Without a doubt, faith covers it with grace. The yoke of slavery to sinful desires hinders your ability to express faith. The wilderness is a place of despair.

James 2:14-26 says, *"What good is it, my brothers and sisters, if someone claims to have faith but has no deeds? Can such faith save them? Suppose a brother or sister is without clothes and daily food. If one of you says to them, Go in peace, keep warm and well fed, but does nothing about their physical needs, what good is it? Similarly, faith without action is meaningless. But someone will say, You have faith; I have deeds. Show me your faith without deeds, and I will show you my faith through my deeds. You believe that there is one God. Good! Even the demons believe this and tremble. You foolish person, do you want evidence that faith without deeds is useless? Was not our father Abraham considered righteous for what he did when he offered his son Isaac on the altar? His actions complemented his faith, making it complete. Abraham fulfilled the Scripture, which states that when he believed in God, God credited him with righteousness and called him his friend. You see, a person is considered righteous based on what they do, not on faith alone. In the same way, was not even Rahab the prostitute considered righteous for what she did when she gave lodging to the spies and sent them off in a different direction? As the body without the Spirit is dead, so faith without deeds is dead."*

In Ephesians 2:10, the Bible tells us that we are God's handiwork. Being God's handiwork necessitates that we conform to His Word, which lives within us. The grace of God is a beautiful attribute that we hold dearly every day of our lives. Considering that we receive it through faith, we should examine our walk to ensure it reflects that faith. The Scriptures describe this battle between flesh and spirit. The Scripture describe this battle between the flesh and the spirit. The mind governed by the flesh is death, whereas the mind governed by the Spirit is life and peace.

A fleshly mind is hostile to God and cannot submit to His law. Those who are in the realm of the flesh cannot please God. If the Spirit of God lives in you, you are in the Spirit realm, not the flesh. Not having the Spirit of Christ means that you do not belong to Him. If Christ is in you, the Spirit gives life because of righteousness, even though sin makes your body die. If His Spirit lives in you, He who raised Christ from the dead will also give life to your mortal bodies.

The flesh's evil desires and temptations govern the mind, drawing us back into sin. The wages of sin are death, and the mind governed by the flesh is death. Whatever sins and evil desires you once indulged in are the strongholds that the enemy will tempt you with going forward. He can use these temptations, as well as the fruits you tasted, to remind you of their temporary pleasures. The deception involves bringing up thoughts of temporary pleasures while hiding the consequences and destructive outcomes that lead to death.

The longer we entertain these thoughts, the more we develop our imagination and ultimately seek to engage in action. During this process, your flesh governs your mind. You must recognize these deceptive tactics in your mind and invoke Jesus to cleanse the temple courts. The prayer of pulling down strongholds, casting down imaginations, and holding thoughts captive under the obedience of Jesus is vital in this war of your mind. The spirit governs the mind, bringing life and peace.

James 4:7-8 says, "*Submit yourselves, then, to God. Resist the devil, and he will flee from you. Come near to God, and He will come near to you. Wash your hands, you sinners, and purify your hearts, you double-minded.*" I'm not afraid to admit that at times I don't want to resist certain temporary pleasures. The flesh will protest, and I can succumb to the deception. I had to endure some hardships to realize that the pleasure and relief weren't worth the cost. The delusion that one more time won't be enough will lead me back to this point repeatedly. At this point, I am inclined to succumb to the delusion of self-blame and lose hope. Then the yoke firmly encircles my neck. What is the purpose of this struggle? The purpose of the enemy's attack is to prevent us from putting our faith into action.

If he can keep me in a state of feeling unworthy and condemned, he's got me right in his snare. God has prepared beneficial works for me in Christ Jesus, but I indulge in evil desires instead. During this struggle, I solely concentrate on myself, avoiding using God as a tool. I will be in the cycle of doing what I don't want to do, feeling awful about doing it, repenting, and repeating. Romans 7:15-25 says, *"I do not understand what I do. I don't do what I desire, but I do what I despise. If I do what I don't want to do, the law is good. As it is, it is no longer I myself who do it; it is sin living in me. For I know that righteousness itself does not dwell in me, that is, in my sinful nature. I desire to do what is good, but I cannot carry it out. Instead of doing what is right, I continue to commit acts of evil. If I do what I don't want to, sin in me does it. Therefore, I observe the following law at work: Although I want to do good, evil is right there with me. For in my inner being, I delight in God's law, but I see another law at work in me, waging war against the law of my mind and making me a prisoner of the law of sin at work within me. What a wretched man I am! Who will save me from this body that is destined for death? Thank you, God, for delivering me through Jesus Christ, our Lord! So then I myself, in my mind, am a slave to God's law, but in my sinful nature, a slave to the law of sin."*

The things I don't want to do are what I do. The things I know better than to do, I will do again. I find myself succumbing to temptation once more, this time in more numerous and distinct forms. This is wicked flesh! At times, it can seem overwhelming, and the enemy's deception attempts to persuade me that it's ineffective and I should resort to other options. Is there a solution to this issue? I've tried to persevere, and it just keeps coming. In these times, what am I saying? Do I express my struggles and worries? Do I buckle the belt of truth around my waist, which holds the breastplate of righteousness in place? Am I holding on to the shield of faith to quell the enemy's fiery darts? Instead of expressing doubt and questioning God during these times, I needed to learn not only about God's armor but also how to wear it every day. It's time that I learn the truth about who I am in Christ.

Doing this changes your mind's atmosphere and enables you to walk in faith. In this life, you will have troubles, as Jesus said, but take heart; I have overcome the world. I had to stop making this life about me and instead step into the power of His resurrection. I had to stop letting the lies of the enemy overwhelm me and speak the truth of God to myself. The enemy is within me. But the God in me is greater than my sin nature. When I fall, I get back up. He will not leave me or forsake me. Speak these truths to yourself. God's Spirit then governs your mind.

This process of sanctification involves renewing the mind and renewing the spirit of your mind. As you learn the Word of God that lives in you, the enemy's lies become less effective, and you see the plots and tactics more clearly. I used to be able to see the plot, but I still became a victim and bought into the lies. It's a daily journey filled with trials and errors, but as my awareness of my identity in Christ grew, so did my strength. It's not that I still don't make poor decisions at times. The difference is that these experiences have helped me follow the Spirit of God, spot my mistakes, and fix them.

The power of it all lies in vocalizing the struggle and deceptive tactics employed against me, thereby alerting others to the enemy's plot. To become a light in the darkness and continue to shine will cause the enemy to flee. Once you begin to use the enemy's own tactics and schemes against him, he will cease to attack you so fervently due to your ability to shine out of the darkness. This entails wielding the spirit's sword. The Spirit of God now governs your mind, using you as a vessel for Jesus. Being alive to the truth of the Word of God allows you to do God's good works. This is utilizing your faith and putting it into action in your life.

Understand that the struggles of your flesh allow your witness and light to shine, demonstrating His strength even in my weakness. As instruments and vessels of God to expose darkness, you have to allow God to use what the enemy meant for evil and turn it for good. This involves harnessing the grace and mercy of God. By utilizing God's gift, which bestows on you what you do not deserve (grace) and shines forth from darkness, God will refrain from bestowing on you what you do deserve (mercy), as long as you allow Him to work in your life. Thank you, Jesus, for your grace and mercy.

Ephesians 4:17-24 says, *"So I tell you this and insist on it in the Lord: you must no longer live as the Gentiles do, in the futility of their thinking." Their ignorance stems from their hearts hardening, darkening their understanding, and separating them from God's life. Having lost all sensitivity, they have surrendered to sensuality, indulging in every impurity and exhibiting greed. However, this is not the way of life you learned when you heard about Christ and received His teachings, which align with the truth found in Jesus. Regarding your previous way of life, you were instructed to discard your old self, which is corrupted by its deceitful desires, cultivate a new mindset, and adopt a new self, created to resemble God in true righteousness and holiness."*

This passage lays out the process of utilizing God's grace and mercy to shine out of darkness. You must demonstrate the principles of your previous lifestyle to allow the Holy Spirit to initiate the process of mind renewal. This way, you will put off your old self and put on the new self, realizing your identity in Jesus. The process appears severe and challenging, emphasizing the battle and its visible aspects. By trusting in Jesus, understanding your sanctification, and focusing on the unseen, you can struggle to produce God's beneficial works.

Jesus' chosen and called disciples serve as an example. Their lives, once filled with tax collection and fishing, underwent a transformation. God used their former way of life to enable them to spread the gospel. Jesus told Peter that he would make him a man's fisherman. Luke 5:1-11 says, *"One day, while Jesus was standing by the lake of Gennesaret, the people were crowding around Him and listening to the Word of God. He saw two boats left at the edge of the water by the fishermen, who were washing their nets. He got into one of the boats, Simon's, and asked him to put out a little from shore. Then He sat down and gave instructions to the people from the boat. After completing His speech, He instructed Simon to venture into deep waters and lower the nets for a catch. Simon answered, 'Master, we've worked hard all night and haven't caught anything. But because you say so, I will let down the nets.' When they had done so, they caught such a large number of fish that their nets began to break. They called for help from their partners in the other boat, who filled both boats to the point of sinking. When Simon Peter saw this, he fell to Jesus' knees and said, 'Go away from me, Lord; I am a sinful man!' All his companions, including Simon's partners, James and John, the sons of Zebedee, were amazed by the fish they caught. Then Jesus said to Simon, 'Don't be afraid; from now on, you will fish for people.' So they pulled their boats up on shore, left everything, and followed Him."*

In the moment, Simon Peter didn't understand Jesus' command to let down their nets for a catch. He had been fishing all night and was tired. Simon Peter's obedience to what appeared to him at the time to be a waste of time, however, was the turning point of his life. Jesus' use of Peter's habitual actions and their connection to His calling is a powerful example for us. The number of fish in the net that caused the boats to sink pales in comparison to the lives we can impact when we allow God to use us. As we come to know Jesus, who sits in the boat of life with us, He asks us to let down the nets in search of a catch. Procrastinate, or blame ourselves for our inability in these moments? Or do we obey Him and become fishers of men in the process?

It takes faith in Jesus' Words, which reside within us, to understand how He can use our imperfections for His purposes. Jesus use of a sinful, unsuccessful fisherman as an example of how to become a fisherman for others is a source of encouragement. We are not too far away from Jesus. The fact that you feel too far gone is confirmation of the deep water. Jesus commanded Simon Peter to dive into the depths. God can use you and your background to reach others. 1 John 1:5–10 says, *"This is the message we have heard from him and declare to you: God is light; in him there is no darkness at all. If we claim to have fellowship with him and yet walk in the darkness, we lie and do not live out the truth. But if we walk in the light, as he is in the light, we have fellowship with one another, and the blood of Jesus, his Son, purifies us from all sin. If we claim to be without sin, we deceive ourselves and the truth is not in us. If we confess our sins, he is faithful and just and will forgive us our sins and purify us from all unrighteousness. If we claim we have not sinned, we make him out to be a liar and his word is not in us."*

Knowing the purpose of Jesus' sacrifice for us makes this passage more clear. God cannot be tempted. Jesus was tempted by the devil. God is light, and there is no darkness in Him. God commands Jesus to bring light from darkness into our hearts. God cannot sin. We made Jesus, who was sinless, sin for us. 2 Corinthians 5:21 says, *"God made him who had no sin to be sin for us, so that in him we might become the righteousness of God."* This makes me truly appreciate Jesus and fully understand His purpose. Jesus is our advocate with the Father. The work of Jesus in our lives will take place despite our sinful nature. This was evident in Peter's cry, "Lord, please leave me. I am a sinful man." When Peter met Jesus, he was not walking in the light. Known tax collectors and notorious sinners ridiculed Jesus for dining with them.

Matthew 9:9–13 says, *"As Jesus went on from there, he saw a man named Matthew sitting at the tax collectors booth. "Follow me," he told Matthew, and Matthew stood up to follow him. While Jesus was having dinner at Matthew's house, many tax collectors and sinners came and ate with Him and His disciples. When the Pharisees noticed this, they questioned His disciples, asking, "Why does your teacher eat with tax collectors and sinners?" When He heard this, Jesus said, 'It is not the healthy who need a doctor, but the sick. But go and learn what this means: I desire mercy, not sacrifice. For I have come not to call the righteous, but sinners."*

My problem was that I didn't understand how the Spirit of God was working in me, even in my mess. Requiring you to clean up before going to Jesus is a major enemy lie. His purpose is to seek and save the lost. He seeks to reconcile us back to God through Himself, purifying us in the process. It's by Faith!

12

To Conquer And Subdue People

Revelation 2:15-16-18 says, *"Likewise, you also have those who hold to the teachings of the Nicolaitans. Repent therefore! Otherwise, I will soon come to you and fight against them with the sword of my mouth. Let anyone with ears hear what the Spirit says to the churches. To the one who is victorious, I will give some of the hidden manna. I will also give that person a white stone with a new name written on it, known only to the one who receives it."*

Jesus warning to the church at Pergamum, which is located in a city also known as Pergamos, was the epicenter of pagan worship. At that time, Pergamos had more shrines and temples built in honor of pagan gods than any other city in the world. In about 29 A.D., Pergamos built a temple in honor of Caesar, the Roman Emperor. In that city, it was mandatory that, no matter what religion or god you served, you pay homage to Caesar at least once a year. Jesus, referring to the city where Satan lives and has his throne, speaks of the evil of Pergamos.

Revelation 2:12-13 says, *"To the angel of the church in Pergamum write: These are the words of him who has the sharp, double-edged sword. I know where you live—where Satan has his throne. Yet you remain true to my name. You did not renounce your faith in me, not even in the days of Antipas, my faithful witness, who was put to death in your city—where Satan lives."* Paganism is any belief or religion outside of Christianity and Judaism. This includes beliefs in Greek gods or goddesses, as well as various forms of occultism. The teaching of the Nicolaitans is a teaching severely rebuked by Jesus, who credits the Church at Ephesus for hating this teaching.

Revelation 2:6 says, *"But you have this in your favor: You hate the practices of the Nicolaitans, which I also hate."* What are the beliefs and practices of the Nicolaitans? It is believed that this teaching derives from Nicolas, who was one of the seven appointed deacons in the first century church. Acts 6:1-7 says, *"In those days when the number of disciples was increasing, the Hellenistic Jews among them complained against the Hebraic Jews because their widows were being overlooked in the daily distribution of food. So the Twelve gathered all the disciples together and said, "It would not be right for us to neglect the ministry of the word of God in order to wait on tables. Brothers and sisters, choose seven men from among you who are known to be full of the Spirit and wisdom. We will turn this responsibility over to them and will give our attention to prayer and the ministry of the word." This proposal pleased the whole group. They chose Stephen, a man full of faith and of the Holy Spirit; also Philip, Procorus, Nicanor, Timon, Parmenas, and Nicolas from Antioch, a convert to Judaism. They presented these men to the apostles, who prayed and laid their hands on them. So the word of God spread. The number of disciples in Jerusalem increased rapidly, and a large number of priests became obedient to the faith."*

In Greek, the name Nicolas is a compound word from Nicos and Laos. The word Nicos means to conquer and subdue. The word Laos means people. The name Nicolas means to conquer and subdue people. According to the passage, Nicolas converted to Judaism. In other translations, he is said to be a Proselyte Jew. This implies that Nicolas, in this instance, began as a Gentile pagan, transitioned to Judaism, underwent circumcision, and later embraced

Christianity. The enemy has the ability to take advantage of the unique blend of our past lives and practices. The enemy uses a similar mixture of our previous experiences and lives to entice us before coming to know Jesus. Whether Nicolas specifically served as the enemy's vessel to conquer and subdue the people is not the issue at hand. The problem is that in the early church, the spirit of evil introduced a doctrine of compromise that is still alive today. Under the grace of Christianity, the doctrine of compromise consisted of pagan rituals mixed with Judaism's practices.

The Nicolaitans practiced and taught pagan rituals on Jewish holy days, claiming grace while believing in Jesus. These pagan rituals consisted of drunken parties and banquets where sexual immorality was rampant. This practice was one of the earliest attempts by the enemy to conquer and subdue the people. The enemy exploited the lust of the flesh in early believers, used intoxication, and dulled the senses to persuade them that their actions were justified by grace, allowing them to continue with their lifestyle. This compromise doctrine, intended to conquer and subdue the people, is still active today. Jesus compared the teaching of the Nicolaitans to that of Baalam, who taught Balak to entice the Israelites to sin, in his warning to the Church in Pergamum.

Revelation 2:14-15 says, *"Nevertheless, I have a few things against you: There are some among you who hold to the teaching of Balaam, who taught Balak to entice the Israelites to sin so that they ate food sacrificed to idols and committed sexual immorality. Likewise, you also have those who hold to the teaching of the Nicolaitans."* Just like the enemy introduced this doctrine of compromise in an attempt to conquer and subdue the people in the early church, that spirit is still active today. The enemy is known to misuse God's Word in his persuasion. Did God really say? This is literally the oldest tactic in the book. Yet, to this day, we still fall for it. I still fall for it; we all do. However, Jesus specifically said, Repent; otherwise, I will soon come to you and fight against them with the sword of my mouth. The Word of God will prevail. It is our choice whether or not we pay attention. Gaining knowledge of God's word is vital in this war of life.

1 Corinthians 10:1-13 says, *"For I do not want you to be ignorant of the fact, brothers and sisters, that our ancestors were all under the cloud and that they all passed through the sea. They were all baptized into Moses in the cloud and in the sea. They all ate the same spiritual food and drank the same spiritual drink; for they drank from the spiritual rock that accompanied them, and that rock was Christ. Nevertheless, God was not pleased with most of them; their bodies were scattered in the wilderness. Now these things occurred as examples to keep us from setting our hearts on evil things as they did. Do not be idolaters, as some of them were; as it is written: "The people sat down to eat and drink and got up to indulge in revelry." We should not commit sexual immorality, as some of them did—and in one day twenty-three thousand of them died. We should not test Christ, as some of them did—and were killed by snakes. And do not grumble, as some of them did—and were killed by the destroying angel. These things happened to them as examples and were written down as warnings for us, on whom the culmination of the ages has come. So, if you think you are standing firm, be careful that you don't fall! No temptation has overtaken you except what is common to mankind. And God is faithful; he will not let you be tempted beyond what you can bear. But when you are tempted, he will also provide a way out so that you can endure it."*

The wilderness is where the enemy does his work. The enemy uses enticement and deception to lure you into the wilderness, a place where he can torture your mind. To conquer and subdue the people. By subduing the people, he can prevent the good works that God has prepared for us to perform, which are an expression of our faith. We receive our salvation through grace and faith. The longer he can torment you and keep your focus on yourself, your problems, your circumstances, and your situation, the more firmly he has you in his snare. The temptation of the flesh is a challenging one to resist. Jesus gives us an insight into this issue and how to overcome it.

Mark 9:42-50 says, *"If anyone causes one of these little ones—those who believe in me—to stumble, it would be better for them if a large millstone were hung around their neck and they were thrown into the sea. If your hand causes you to stumble, cut it off. It is better for you to enter life maimed than with two hands to go into hell, where the fire never goes out. And if your foot causes you to stumble, cut it off. It is better for you to enter life crippled than to have two feet and be thrown into hell. And if your eye causes you to stumble, pluck it out. It is better for you to enter the kingdom of God with one eye than to have two eyes and be thrown into hell, where "the worms that eat them do not die, and the fire is not quenched.' Everyone will be salted with fire. "Salt is good, but if it loses its saltiness, how can you make it salty again? Have salt among yourselves, and be at peace with each other."*

Jesus begins this particular lesson with a warning against those who cause those who believe in Him to stumble. It is wise to observe our actions and how they affect or lead others into error. Placing a millstone around their necks and tossing it into the sea is a better outcome for them than trying to use Christ in this situation. This is not a laughing matter. Jesus then gives us insight into preventative measures to take if our actions cause us to stumble. Our hands represent our work. If our efforts are causing us to stumble, cut them off. Look for preventative measures in this area of your life.

You need a partner who will hold you accountable for achieving your goals. Jesus predicted that fire would save everyone. Have salt among yourselves. Pray about this issue and seek help from someone who understands what is causing you to stumble and can assist you. It's preferable to suffer this kind of injury than to let your mistakes dictate your actions. Your foot symbolizes the places you go. If the places you are going are causing you to stumble, look for other options and cut them off. Communicate openly with those in your life, let them know that you are experiencing temptation in this area, and sever the connection. It's preferable to suffer harm in this area than to persist in making mistakes.

The eyes are clearly visible. What are we observing and consuming that nourishes our desires and lures us in? Take preventative measures and be transparent with the people in your life. If you struggle with porn and things online, share your password to your email with an accountability partner. Keeping in mind that someone is monitoring what you are viewing will help you avoid the things that lead to mistakes. Keep in mind, it's preferable to sustain injuries in this area than to persist in your mistake, thereby providing the enemy with a foothold and maintaining your subjugation.

We must take inventory of our lives and listen to God's Spirit. What is holding us back? How can I avoid what is causing me to stumble? What needs to be cut off? Taking these steps, being honest with yourself, and seeking answers from Jesus is a big step. Being obedient means paying attention to the Spirit as He provides you with insight and clarity, and then putting these truths into practice. Understand what the enemy is using to conquer and subdue you in your life. Then, take the preventative measures taught by Jesus and apply them to your life. He cares for you and loves you. Trust Him.

The enemy's plan to conquer and subdue the people is also an organizational attempt. The principalities and powers manipulate those in the physical world to carry out their intentions. Although social media serves as a means to stay connected with friends and family, the enemy uses it as a tool to incite evil desires. Lust, pride, envy, hatred, slander, gossip, lies, and basically every evil imaginable are at your disposal on social media in the comfort of your own home. The doctrine of compromise at work involves deceiving popular opinion and letting your views of culture and what's popular influence you.

The opinions and stories of people's circumstances will cause you to rethink: did God really say this was evil? Listening to touching stories that prey on your compassion will attempt to divert your attention from what God actually says about certain things. Do not be deceived. Pay attention to the times we are living in and how the enemy is using them. Observe the plot carefully to avoid falling prey to his schemes. At the time of Jesus' warning to the Church in Pergamum, the people of the city built temples and shrines to pagan gods and goddesses. They didn't care what religion or god you served; just pay homage to Caesar once a year. This level of compromise was enough to subdue the people.

Paying homage once. That same spirit of compromise came to fruition by instituting Easter on the Day of the Resurrection of our Lord Jesus. Estre, a pagan goddess of fertility, inspired the name of Easter. This is a prime illustration of the Nicolaitans' teachings. They use Easter eggs as a symbol of fertility. They also use the eastern bunny, one of the world's most reproductive animals. They use these paganism symbols to mock and distract from the holy day of Jesus' Resurrection. The foundation of our faith They do this right in front of our faces. They popularize it by making it seem harmless. Children participate in Easter egg hunts and receive Easter baskets filled with candy. Churches participate in these practices and promote them, oblivious to the mockery of their own intentions. The war is real.

The issue does not lie with the institution or group of people that organized the change from holy days to holidays. The problem is that the principality and powers of wickedness are obvious. The fleshly vessels carrying out this wickedness are not the enemy. They were deceived; it seems harmless, right? Due to ignorance, individuals engage in this mockery, passing it down from generation to generation. It's a wake-up call to all of us. Deception will always appear harmless. The powers of spiritual wickedness are rampant, and the evidence is overwhelming. It's time to see it for what it truly is and take a personal inventory of our lives. What hidden idols have we blindly worshipped?

Hosea 4:6-8 says, *"My people are destroyed from lack of knowledge."Because you have rejected knowledge, I also reject you as my priests; because you have ignored the law of your God, I also will ignore your children. The more priests there were, the more they sinned against me; they exchanged their glorious God for something disgraceful. They feed on the sins of my people and relish their wickedness."*

In the Book of Daniel, we learn of three men named Shadrach, Meshach, and Abednego. In this time of Scripture, Nebuchadnezzar, king of Babylon, had come to Jerusalem and besieged it, and the Lord delivered it into his hands. Nebuchadnezzar had taken captive some of the Israelites and ordered his chief to select some of them to bring into the king's service. Shadrach, Meshach, and Abednego were selected. During this time, Nebuchadnezzar had made an image of gold about ninety feet high and nine feet wide. He placed it on the plain of Dura in the province of Babylon. Nebuchadnezzar then summoned all the satraps, treasurers, prefects, governors, judges, and all other provincial officials to come to the dedication of the image he had set up. Nebuchadnezzar declared that upon hearing the music, everyone was to fall down and worship the gold image, and anyone who refused would face immediate destruction in a blazing furnace.

Nebuchadnezzar received reports that some Jews he had chosen to serve in Babylon had disregarded his decree and worshipped the image of gold. Nebuchadnezzar was furious with rage and summoned Shadrach, Meshach, and Abednego. Nebuchadnezzar personally repeated his command to them, making sure they understood the consequences if they refused to worship the image of gold.

Daniel 3:16-30 says, *"Shadrach, Meshach and Abednego replied to him, "King Nebuchadnezzar, we do not need to defend ourselves before you in this matter. If we are thrown into the blazing furnace, the God we serve is able to deliver us from it, and he will deliver us from Your Majesty's hand. But even if he does not, we want you to know, Your Majesty, that we will not serve your gods or worship the image of gold you have set up." Then Nebuchadnezzar was furious with Shadrach, Meshach and Abednego, and his attitude toward them changed. He ordered the furnace heated seven times hotter than usual and commanded some of the strongest soldiers in his army to tie up Shadrach, Meshach and Abednego and throw them into the blazing furnace. So these men, wearing their robes, trousers, turbans and other clothes, were bound and thrown into the blazing furnace. The king's command was so urgent and the furnace so hot that the flames of the fire killed the soldiers who took up Shadrach, Meshach and Abednego, and these three men, firmly tied, fell into the blazing furnace. Then King Nebuchadnezzar leaped to his feet in amazement and asked his advisers, "Weren't there three men that we tied up and threw into the fire? They replied, "Certainly, Your Majesty." He said, "Look! I see four men walking around in the fire, unbound and unharmed, and the fourth looks like a son of the gods." Nebuchadnezzar then approached the opening of the blazing furnace and shouted, "Shadrach, Meshach and Abednego, servants of the Most High God, come out! Come here! So Shadrach, Meshach and Abednego came out of the fire, and the satraps, prefects, governors and royal advisers crowded around them. They saw that the fire had not harmed their bodies, nor was a hair of their heads singed; their robes were not scorched, and there was no smell of fire on them. Then Nebuchadnezzar said, "Praise be to the God of Shadrach, Meshach and Abednego, who has sent his angel and rescued his servants! They trusted in him and defied the king's command and were willing to give up their lives rather than serve or worship any god except their own God. Therefore I decree that the people of any nation or language who say anything against the God of Shadrach, Meshach and Abednego be cut into pieces and their houses be turned into piles of rubble, for no other god can save in this way. Then the king promoted Shadrach, Meshach and Abednego in the province of Babylon."*

Although refusing to compromise can get you through the fire, we have a God who will walk us through it. The status of Shadrach, Meshach, and Abednego was in jeopardy with the king. They could have compromised and kept their status. It appeared they would lose not only their status but also their lives if they did not compromise. However, in the face of apparent death, they held their faith that God was able to deliver them. Their obedience and trust in God brought them promotion instead of keeping their status. Because of their obedience, God used the king who was against them to promote them. God is truly in control!

If Shadrach, Meshach, and Abednego had surrendered, they would have faced defeat and subjugation. The Most High would not have rewarded them or shown them favor. Despite the necessity of enduring hardships to demonstrate God's favor, being in a state of compromise prevents any of this from happening. Obedience is necessary to show God's strength and power in the face of adversity, which opens the door to favor with men.

Proverbs 3:3-4 says, *"Let love and faithfulness never leave you; bind them around your neck, write them on the tablet of your heart. Then you will win favor and a good name in the sight of God and man."* The pressures of popular opinion and what's trending can lead to a worldly view of a compromised state. This is just one of the many risks associated with social media. We may find ourselves agreeing with actions that God specifically instructs us against. In doing this, we fail to understand and underestimate the influence of others, which causes them to stumble as well. Jesus issued a clear and grave warning to those who lead His followers astray. We have become so relaxed about our religion that our relationship has stalled. Yet here I am eating, drinking, and getting up to indulge in revelry. Jesus says, Therefore, repent!

When I began to realize these truths about God and how I'd utterly failed in miserable ways, I couldn't help but cry out to Jesus. Woe is me, Lord, a man with unclean lips! Help my unbelief! Restore me to alignment with You and guide my ways. No longer will I live a conquered and subdued life. Use me, Lord; send me, and I will go. Psalm 32:3-7 says, *"When I kept silent, my bones wasted away through my groaning all day long. For day and night your hand was heavy on me; my strength was sapped as in the heat of summer. Then I acknowledged my sin to you and did not cover up my iniquity. I said, "I will confess my transgressions to the Lord."And you forgave the guilt of my sin. Therefore let all the faithful pray to you while you may be found; surely the rising of the mighty waters will not reach them. You are my hiding place; you will protect me from trouble and surround me with songs of deliverance."*

I now understand the risks associated with compromise and submission. Being in this state will limit my experience of seeing God work in my life. Does maintaining my current status in the eyes of the public and society justify the price of obedience and advancement? The sight of the blazing furnace was eerie and intimidating. The fire devoured the soldiers who escorted them to it. It was hot! Maintaining your integrity in front of God can be challenging and unpopular. Experiencing His deliverance is worth it.

13

The Out Pouring

Acts 2:17-18 says, *"In the last days, God says, I will pour out my Spirit on all people. Your sons and daughters will prophesy, your young men will see visions, your old men will dream dreams. Even on my servants, both men and women, I will pour out my Spirit in those days, and they will prophesy."* Peter spoke the words of Prophet Joel in response to the crowd's reaction on the Day of Pentecost. While the people were speaking in tongues and prophesying, those in the crowd were saying they must be drunk. The Holy Spirit is pouring out today, just as He did at Pentecost. The outpouring of God's Spirit is upon us. With all the evil in this world, there is still an outpouring taking place.

Some have been unable to fully experience this gift due to a lack of faith stemming from their focus on the visible. The sound of a powerful, rushing, and violent wind is terrifying. As the Bible describes, the sound of what appeared to be tongues of fire separating and coming to rest on each of them adds to the terrifying atmosphere. This wasn't a dove that flew over them; this was an outpouring of God's spirit and power.

Acts 2:2-3 says, *"Suddenly a sound like the blowing of a violent wind came from heaven and filled the whole house where they were sitting. They saw what seemed to be tongues of fire that separated and came to rest on each of them.”* Peter began to explain to the crowds of people, who were witnessing those filled with the Holy Spirit and speaking in tongues, that Jesus, the crucified and raised from the dead, is the Lord and Messiah. People in the crowd were bewildered and asked, What shall we do?

Acts 2:38-41 says, *“Peter replied, “Repent and be baptized, every one of you, in the name of Jesus Christ for the forgiveness of your sins. And you will receive the gift of the Holy Spirit. The promise is for you and your children and for all who are far off—for all whom the Lord our God will call.” With many other words he warned them; and he pleaded with them, “Save yourselves from this corrupt generation.” Those who accepted his message were baptized, and about three thousand were added to their number that day.”* I admit that I have always been skeptical of the operations of the Holy Spirit. I remember, as a child, attending church. I witnessed people speaking in tongues, and then someone would interpret the message. I was unable to comprehend the meaning behind all of this. I lacked comprehension and was perplexed by everything. I grew up attending a Pentecostal church. As people were singing and worshiping, some would get excited and run around the building, shouting. As a child, I couldn’t help but laugh at what I was seeing. It was funny, and as I grew older, my skepticism became unbelief in it all. I didn’t understand spiritual truths at all.

Then, catastrophe struck my life. Hopelessness and despair tossed me like winds and waves. Through it all, I knew God had seen me, and He knew what happened. I continued to act in accordance with my understanding of the situation. I relied on drugs and self-medication to endure each day. Time went on, but I still believed that God knew my situation and that I would be OK. When circumstances in prison finally got me to a place where I had nowhere else to turn, I cried out to Jesus. I wept and wept, and I gave it all to Him. At that moment, I encountered the Holy Spirit. I didn’t understand it then, but it was happening. I just felt peace.

Over the next few years, I didn't understand how the Holy Spirit was working in me. I just felt different. Even through all my mistakes, relapses, and setbacks, I didn't understand how the Holy Spirit was working in me. When I would attend certain chapel services, I could feel the Spirit of God in that place, and I began to realize the Spirit lived in me. Despite all the setbacks, I began to hear His voice and feel His urging to refrain from certain actions, and Scriptures began to come to mind. I begin to watch how certain things will line up in my path for me to experience events. When I couldn't access the places or activities I desired, I would become frustrated. Later, I learned about the events in the area I was attempting to visit, and I understood that I was under protection.

This process of beginning to understand the functions of the Holy Spirit in my life took time. I'm a stubborn person who often disobeyed and brought hardship upon myself. However, the Holy Spirit continued to guide me during those challenging times. He picked me up and brought me through. I began to discuss spiritual truths with other people and realized how they had similar experiences. The Holy Spirit was not what I had pictured in my mind. My perception of the Holy Spirit was way off.

The more I grew in my knowledge of Jesus and the Word of God, the more I became aware of the Holy Spirit in me. The more I became aware of the Holy Spirit within me, the more I recognized His voice. I could be listening to the radio or watching TV and seeing a commercial talking about a product, but something they say speaks directly to me. These times excite me, and seeing God in everything comforts me. Hearing a particular song at the right time and feeling God's presence is priceless. It's a wonderful feeling to know God is with you. Being in error, calling back out to Him, and experiencing His faithfulness and love when I strayed away in disobedience is amazing.

Having these experiences, and then realizing he wants to use you, is a game changer. Then all my flaws and feelings of unworthiness come to the surface. How can you use me? Lord, this is a question I asked from a place of doubt. I'm not qualified to preach. I'm not competent enough to do it. I have never been comfortable standing and talking in front of people. Until I stepped out in faith. It took time for me to grow in Him and realize it was about Him, not me. I fully understand that, on my own, I'm a mess. But fully understanding who He is in you takes it to another level. Growing in relationship with Jesus, He teaches you about you and how you can help those like you through Him who lives in you. It's truly an amazing journey full of ups and downs, but He's with you through it all.

During Jesus' time on earth with His disciples, He sent them out into Israel and gave them authority to drive out impure spirits and heal every disease and sickness. Jesus gave them many instructions on how to deal with people and how to handle situations. Matthew 10:24-33 says, *"The student is not above the teacher, nor a servant above his master. It is enough for students to be like their teachers, and servants like their masters. If the head of the house has been called Beelzebul, how much more the members of his household!"So do not be afraid of them, for there is nothing concealed that will not be disclosed, or hidden that will not be made known. What I tell you in the dark, speak in the daylight; what is whispered in your ear, proclaim from the roofs. Do not be afraid of those who kill the body but cannot kill the soul. Rather, be afraid of the One who can destroy both soul and body in hell. Are not two sparrows sold for a penny? Yet not one of them will fall to the ground outside your Father's care. And even the very hairs of your head are all numbered. So don't be afraid; you are worth more than many sparrows. "Whoever acknowledges me before others, I will also acknowledge before my Father in heaven. But whoever disowns me before others, I will disown before my Father in heaven."*

Jesus sending out the Twelve Disciples allowed them to gain the needed experience for their task of spreading the Gospel. The disciples were unaware of their purpose, which was to come in the future. They made preparations for their destiny. Jesus instructed them, saying, Don't be afraid. Nothing remains hidden that we won't reveal, and nothing remains hidden that we won't reveal. Jesus said, What I tell you in the dark, make known in the daylight, and what He whispers in their ears, proclaim from the roofs. This truth still stands for us today. The work of the Holy Spirit in our lives teaches us these truths.

For a long time, I couldn't see what was happening to me. I was unaware of His work taking place in my life. The outpouring of His Spirit was upon me, and I wasn't grasping the truth. Looking back, I can clearly perceive the lessons I learned during the storm. I was being equipped. The Holy Spirit, the counselor, was at work. Luke 22:31-32 says, *"Simon, Simon, Satan has asked to sift all of you as wheat. But I have prayed for you, Simon, that your faith may not fail. And when you have turned back, strengthen your brothers."*

Satan will sift you like wheat. This requires going through some things. Yet Jesus, praying that his faith may not fail, suggests that it be tested. It sounds like a process we are all familiar with. What is the purpose behind all of this? Jesus responds by saying, And when you have turned back, strengthen your brothers. Utilize the wisdom and knowledge gained from the storm's process to shine a light into darkness. This is only possible with the Holy Spirit, a Comforter and Counselor. John 14:26 says, *"But the Advocate, the Holy Spirit, whom the Father will send in my name, will teach you all things and will remind you of everything I have said to you."*

Before King Agrippa recounted his experience and encounter with Jesus on the road to Damascus, Paul made his case. Paul recounted his conversation with Jesus after seeing his glorious light. Jesus told Paul the following: Acts 26:17-18 says, *"I will rescue you from your own people and from the Gentiles. I am sending you to them to open their eyes and turn them from darkness to light, and from the power of Satan to God, so that they may receive forgiveness of sins and a place among those who are sanctified by faith in me."*

The Holy Spirit works in our lives to sanctify us, allowing us to receive forgiveness for our sins and a place among those who have placed their faith in Me. This sanctification feels as though I am different from others and that the Holy Spirit is not present within me. The process is the work of the Holy Spirit in our lives. I couldn't understand the difference between the gifts of the Spirit and its workings in me. My lack of knowledge and understanding in this capacity confused me. I would often feel as though I am different from others and that the Holy Spirit is not present within me. I've been unaware of the Holy Spirit's presence all along. He holds a position among those who are purifying themselves through faith in Jesus.

2 Thessalonians 2:13–14 says, *"But we ought always to thank God for you, brothers and sisters loved by the Lord, because God chose you as first fruits to be saved through the sanctifying work of the Spirit and through belief in the truth. He called you to this through our gospel, that you might share in the glory of our Lord Jesus Christ."* 1 Thessalonians 5:23 says, *"May God himself, the God of peace, sanctify you through and through. May your whole spirit, soul and body be kept blameless at the coming of our Lord Jesus Christ."*

Because I wasn't operating through the gifts of the Spirit, I felt that I wasn't full of the Holy Spirit. I experienced a shift and sensed guidance, yet I remained perplexed. The Holy Spirit's refining and sanctifying work was very alive and working in me. Many aspects of my thinking, habits, addictions, character, and entire being underwent significant transformation. This is the sanctifying process of being born again. A new creature. It doesn't happen overnight; it requires you to take up your cross and follow Him. It doesn't happen overnight; it requires you to take up your cross and follow Him. Jesus explained this truth to Nicodemus, who came and met Jesus one night. Nicodemus, a Pharisee, found himself drawn to learn more about Jesus.

John 3:1-8 says, *"Now there was a Pharisee, a man named Nicodemus who was a member of the Jewish ruling council. He came to Jesus at night and said, "Rabbi, we know that you are a teacher who has come from God. For no one could perform the signs you are doing if God were not with him." Jesus replied, "Very truly I tell you, no one can see the kingdom of God unless they are born again. "How can someone be born when they are old?" Nicodemus asked. "Surely they cannot enter a second time into their mother's womb to be born!" Jesus answered, "Very truly I tell you, no one can enter the kingdom of God unless they are born of water and the Spirit. Flesh gives birth to flesh, but the Spirit gives birth to spirit. You should not be surprised at my saying, 'You must be born again.' The wind blows wherever it pleases. You hear its sound, but you cannot tell where it comes from or where it is going. So it is with everyone born of the Spirit."*

As I came to understand the process of sanctification and the work of the Holy Spirit in me, I began to see things differently. I am born again. This flesh has given birth to flesh, and the Spirit has given birth to my spirit. Everything I've learned from my flesh must now adapt to the Spirit within me. This explains why some things I used to indulge in do not feel the same. I can't enjoy the temporary pleasure like I once did. It grieves the spirit in me. The more I become knowledgeable of God's Word, the more I enable the Spirit to lead me into all truth.

The struggle between the flesh and the spirit that lives in me is not to punish my efforts to be born again. It's the equipping of God's wisdom, knowledge, and understanding to shine out of darkness. Being born again means you have to grow. Growing pains take place. Disobedience and chastening take place. Learning from mistakes and gaining clarity will take place. None of it takes place without faith. Bad days and frustrations can lead us to develop negative attitudes towards others or engage in arguments. Afterwards, the workings of the Holy Spirit in you will show you your error and draw you back to that person to make things right. As we listen to the Spirit showing us areas we need to work on, clarity will come.

When you don't get it right, don't worry; another opportunity is coming. This process sharpens our character. This essential quality serves as a powerful tool. We all fail these tests, but improving through failure leads to victory through defeat. Through this process, heeding the guidance of the Holy Spirit will teach you about yourself so that you can help those with anger issues. You should learn a lesson from every struggle for your own benefit. Romans 8:28 says, *"And we know that in all things God works for the good of those who love Him, who have been called according to His purpose."*

We all enjoy reading this Scripture, which says that despite our actions and behavior, God is going to make it for our good. The danger in thinking this way is the failure to realize we are God's vessels. Creating enemies and harboring grudges obstruct any positive outcomes. The Scripture plainly says to those who love Him: Jesus said, If you love Him, keep His commands. John 14:15 says, *"If you love me, keep my commands."* John 15:9-12 says, *"As the Father has loved me, so have I loved you. Now remain in my love. If you keep my commands, you will remain in my love, just as I have kept my Father's commands and remain in his love. I have told you this so that my joy may be in you and that your joy may be complete. My command is this: Love each other as I have loved you."*

If a spirit is leading you contrary to this truth, it is not the Holy Spirit. God instructs us to test the spirits to determine their authenticity. 1 John 4:1 says, *"Dear friends, do not believe every spirit, but test the spirits to see whether they are from God, because many false prophets have gone out into the world."* The Holy Spirit will lead you into all truth. Your failure to know the truth opens the door for the enemy to draw you into error. Jesus said you will know the truth, and the truth will set you free. Knowing the truth about God enables the Holy Spirit to work in you and dispels the lies of the enemy. In doing so, you will allow God to use what was meant for evil and use it for good. Jesus' temptation in the wilderness beautifully displayed this truth.

Luke 4:1–12 says, *"Jesus, full of the Holy Spirit, left the Jordan and was led by the Spirit into the wilderness, where for forty days he was tempted by the devil. He ate nothing during those days, and at the end of them he was hungry. The devil said to him, "If you are the Son of God, tell this stone to become bread."Jesus answered, "It is written: 'Man shall not live on bread alone."The devil led him up to a high place and showed him in an instant all the kingdoms of the world. And he said to him, "I will give you all their authority and splendor; it has been given to me, and I can give it to anyone I want to. If you worship me, it will all be yours." Jesus answered, "It is written: 'Worship the Lord your God and serve him only." The devil led him to Jerusalem and had him stand on the highest point of the temple. "If you are the Son of God," he said, "throw yourself down from here. For it is written: "He will command his angels concerning you to guard you carefully; they will lift you up in their hands, so that you will not strike your foot against a stone." Jesus answered, "It is said: 'Do not put the Lord your God to the test."*

Jesus, full of the Holy Spirit, was able to use truth to combat the temptation of the enemy. The devil tempted Jesus with bread. A short time later, Jesus fed the five thousand with five loaves of bread and two fish. Jesus is the bread of life. The bread from heaven Jesus utilized the temptation He faced to accomplish His mission. The devil used earthly authority to tempt Jesus.

Jesus gave His disciples authority over impure spirits and healed disease and sickness. All authority in heaven, earth, and under the earth came to Jesus. We, as believers, have authority in His name on earth today.

The devil used status and protection to tempt Jesus. Jesus sits at the Father's right hand. He is our mediator and advocate with the Father. He served as a devoted high priest, enduring every temptation to view us with empathy. It's comforting to know that God calls the foolish things in this world to confound the wise. lowly in heart. If you've been broken down and your life shattered, Jesus is the answer. If you are a product of negligent decisions and a shameful past, Jesus is the answer. Invoke His name and surrender to the outpouring of His Spirit. He specializes in using the broken past and your pain to serve His purpose moving forward.

1 Corinthians 1:26–30 says, *"Brothers and sisters, think of what you were when you were called. Not many of you were wise by human standards; not many were influential; not many were of noble birth. But God chose the foolish things of the world to shame the wise; God chose the weak things of the world to shame the strong. God chose the lowly things of this world and the despised things—and the things that are not—to nullify the things that are, so that no one may boast before him. It is because of him that you are in Christ Jesus, who has become for us wisdom from God—that is, our righteousness, holiness and redemption."* Therefore, the scripture states, "Let the one who boasts boast in the Lord."

The outpouring of His Spirit is upon us. Take heart, knowing that He is with you. Allow His Spirit to sanctify you. Look for His guidance and listen to His voice. I was in that cell that night, and I cried out to Jesus. I was weeping, and a light shone in my cell. It wasn't a blinding light, but there was no electricity in my cell. I was in darkness. As I cried out to him, a light illuminated me. I felt a peace in that moment that I cannot explain. In pure brokenness and despair, I called upon Him fully with everything in me. I wasn't familiar with stories in the Bible at the time. I had a Bible that I hid contraband in, but I never read it.

The following day, as I started reading, a breeze would blow through my window, causing the pages to turn as I read. I would begin reading, and as I did, the breeze would flip the pages and stop. I could feel His presence beside me so strongly. I had never fasted before, and I went on a three-day fast. Ever since that night, I have paid attention to the lights. If I'm in deep thought about something, sometimes I can see a light. Whether it's a reflection, a flickering light in the dorm, or anything else, I know that God communicates with me through light. I was hesitant to write about this in the book, but lightning flashed through my window. I don't care who believes me or who thinks I'm crazy. I'm writing about my experiences with Jesus.

I came across the teachings of Urim and Thummin, and when I read about them, I was amazed. God has a history of using lights to communicate with His people. I say this to reassure those who have had similar experiences with God, not to let others' opinions discourage how the Lord communicates with you. Whether or not they believe you or think you are crazy, It will not impact how God communicates with you. Praise his name. Give him glory. Wherever you are in your walk with Jesus, continue to grow in His Word that lives in you. Learn to listen and obey the Holy Spirit. When you slip and make bad decisions, listen to the counselor, not the condemner. Learn from every mistake and get back up again. Communicate with him. The Holy Spirit's work revolves around relationships with Jesus. Personally growing in him. The gifts of the Spirit will come as you continue to grow in Him. Hallelujah!

14

Take Your Position

STAND FIRM

2 Chronicles 20:17 says, *"You will not have to fight this battle. Take up your positions; stand firm and see the deliverance the Lord will give you, Judah and Jerusalem. Do not be afraid; do not be discouraged. Go out to face them tomorrow, and the Lord will be with you."* The Lord will be with you. Although the battle is not ours, we do have to take our positions and stand firm. This scripture alerts Jehoshaphat to the approaching vast army. Hearing this news, Jehoshaphat proclaimed a fast throughout Judah and inquired of the Lord. Like Jehoshaphat, we face a vast army seeking to kill, steal, and destroy us. The Lord instructed Jehoshaphat to take his position and stand firm. The Lord declares this same proclamation over each of us.

The enemy's attempts to sway our positioning so that we stumble are his only chance against us. Taking our position and standing firm places the battle in the Lord's hands. The enemy is powerless to resist the Lord's might. As a result, his attack contradicts our position. The testing of faith in 2 Chronicles 20:20 says, *"Early in the morning they left for the Desert of Tekoa. As they set out, Jehoshaphat stood and said, "Listen to me, Judah and people of Jerusalem! Have faith in the Lord your God and you will be upheld; have faith in his prophets and you will be successful."*

This is a tangible manifestation of what we are striving for in the Spirit today. The people knew they stood no chance of defeating this vast army. All they had was faith in the Lord's Word on their side. That's it! They lacked the physical weapons necessary to defeat this army. They were helpless. The threats coming against them, as well as the sight of this army, were terrifying. They didn't have the Holy Spirit in them as a people. All they had was the Word of the Lord spoken through the Prophet to stand on. They were familiar with the history of God delivering their ancestors from slavery in Egypt.

They had not personally experienced the apparent disaster and defeat. While taking their positions and standing firm on the Word of the Lord, the people expressed their faith. 2 Chronicles 20:21–24 says, *"After consulting the people, Jehoshaphat appointed men to sing to the Lord and to praise him for the splendor of his holiness as they went out at the head of the army, saying: "Give thanks to the Lord, for his love endures forever." As they began to sing and praise, the Lord set ambushes against the men of Ammon and Moab and Mount Seir who were invading Judah, and they were defeated. The Ammonites and Moabites rose up against the men from Mount Seir to destroy and annihilate them. After they finished slaughtering the men from Seir, they helped to destroy one another. When the men of Judah came to the place that overlooks the desert and looked toward the vast army, they saw only dead bodies lying on the ground; no one had escaped."*

By taking their positions and standing firm on the Word of the Lord, they witnessed the deliverance of the Lord. Expressing their faith by praising God for His promise to deliver activated God to deliver. In the face of apparent death and destruction, they remained true to His promise. Through faith in His word, they were able to praise Him in the middle of the storm. When it looks like all of hell is coming against you. There is an opportunity to compromise or to stand firm.

The taking of your positions is your standing. Are you standing on the promises of His Word to deliver or on the compromise of the enemy to settle for less? Taking the position of standing on God's Word and expressing faith will not fail you. He will see you through, and you will witness the Lord's deliverance. God rewarded His people for their faith. 2 Chronicles 20:25 says, *"So Jehoshaphat and his men went to carry off their plunder, and they found among them a great amount of equipment and clothing and also articles of value—more than they could take away. There was so much plunder that it took three days to collect it."* Not only did the Lord set ambushes against their enemies, but He also destroyed them.

He allowed his people to plunder their possessions to meet their needs and prosper. They stood firm against all odds while believing in His word. Today, we have the luxury of the Holy Spirit in us, along with the written Word of God to study. Walking with Jesus, we cannot lose. God's favor didn't prevent a vast army from coming against Jehoshaphat. It provided an opportunity to express faith in His word. The plundering of the enemy's spoil is beneficial to your calling and purpose in Him. This is why it is considered pure joy when faced with trials. It is an opportunity to express your faith.

When you start winning battles by taking your position and standing firm, you gain a reputation among the enemy. 2 Chronicles 20:29–30 says, *"The fear of God came on all the surrounding kingdoms when they heard how the Lord had fought against the enemies of Israel. And the kingdom of Jehoshaphat was at peace, for his God had given him rest on every side."* To become more than a conqueror, you must take your position and stand firm. The God of Peace will give you His peace. The tests become a testimony to His love, which endures forever.

Romans 8:36-39 says, *"As it is written: "For your sake we face death all day long; we are considered as sheep to be slaughtered." No, in all these things we are more than conquerors through him who loved us. For I am convinced that neither death nor life, neither angels nor demons, neither the present nor the future, nor any powers, neither height nor depth, nor anything else in all creation, will be able to separate us from the love of God that is in Christ Jesus our Lord."* The power is in the name of Jesus. One thing the enemy wants you to not know is the power of Jesus' name. This is your identity as a believer. Jesus lives in you. Speak his name.

Ephesians 1:18-23 says, *"I pray that the eyes of your heart may be enlightened in order that you may know the hope to which he has called you, the riches of his glorious inheritance in his holy people and his incomparably great power for us who believe. That power is the same as the mighty strength he exerted when he raised Christ from the dead and seated him at his right hand in the heavenly realms, far above all rule and authority, power and dominion, and every name that is invoked, not only in the present age but also in the one to come. And God placed all things under his feet and appointed him to be head over everything for the church, which is his body, the fullness of him who fills everything in every way."*

Jesus went to the cross and paid the debt of sin for us. Therefore, it is through faith in Jesus that we have grace. This grace takes away the power of sin that the devil uses. The wages of sin are death. Through Jesus, we have life. Grace and life, through faith in Jesus, remove the sting of death, the wages of sin. The power of the cross, and what it meant, is eternal life. The Resurrection of Jesus empowers His Sacrifice as Life. Therefore, because He lives, we will also live through faith in Him. The only avenue the enemy has against us is the attack on our faith, through which we obtain grace.

1 Corinthians 15:56–58 says, *"The sting of death is sin, and the power of sin is the*

law. But thanks be to God! He gives us the victory through our Lord Jesus Christ. Therefore, my dear brothers and sisters, stand firm. Let nothing move you. Always give yourselves fully to the work of the Lord, because you know that your labor in the Lord is not in vain." I had to learn the importance of not just knowing Jesus and believing in His finished work on the cross. I had to learn about my relationship with God and His work in me. It's one thing to say that I believe and go about my life with no regard for His work in me. It's another reason for me to believe and grow with Him.

There is authority in His name; make no mistake about it. However, only utilizing His authority without regard for His work places you in jeopardy of Him not knowing you on the day of judgment. Matthew 7:21-23 says, *"Not everyone who says to me, 'Lord, Lord,' will enter the kingdom of heaven, but only the one who does the will of my Father who is in heaven. Many will say to me on that day, 'Lord, Lord, did we not prophesy in your name and in your name drive out demons and in your name perform many miracles?' Then I will tell them plainly, 'I never knew you. Away from me, you evildoers!"*Learning from what Jesus says in this text is tremendously important. Knowing Him and the Works in His Name is not beneficial enough. He must know you. Having a relationship with him and allowing him to work in your life are keys. We cannot overstate the importance of listening to the Holy Spirit and understanding what it means to be born again. It's a process of growth as you believe in Him, allowing Him to transform and utilize you. Allowing Jesus to work in your life will reveal that your struggles will fit you to honor Him.

2 Timothy 2:20–22 says, *"In a large house there are articles not only of gold and silver, but also of wood and clay; some are for special purposes and some for common use. Those who cleanse themselves from the latter will be instruments for special purposes, made holy, useful to the Master and prepared to do any good work. Flee the evil desires of youth and pursue righteousness, faith, love and peace,*

along with those who call on the Lord out of a pure heart." Becoming His vessel is the best way to ensure your relationship with Jesus. Being fit for the master's use.

2 Timothy 2:3–7 says, *"Join with me in suffering, like a good soldier of Christ Jesus. No one serving as a soldier gets entangled in civilian affairs, but rather tries to please his commanding officer. Similarly, anyone who competes as an athlete does not receive the victor's crown except by competing according to the rules. The hardworking farmer should be the first to receive a share of the crops. Reflect on what I am saying, for the Lord will give you insight into all this."* The armor of God is our spiritual garment as soldiers of Jesus. Utilizing the armor's intended purpose is essential for securing our positions and maintaining our firmness. Listen to his voice as he guides you. He will make his words known to you.

Proverbs 1:23 says, *"Repent at my rebuke! Then I will pour out my thoughts to you, I will make known to you my teachings."* Our calling is to remain uncompromising and unconquered. The armor of God equips us as Christ's soldiers. The principalities and powers have taken up territory in the cities. Strongholds of spiritual wickedness exist in certain areas, blinding and deceiving human vessels to carry out their commands. Look at what plagues different areas. It's not hidden. It's right in front of our eyes. Yet I can become blinded as well by falling into deception and becoming subdued. The enemy's plot aims to subdue the elders while poisoning the youth's minds. As you read these words, it's playing out in our culture.

As people and soldiers of Christ, we must take seriously the epidemic of the enemy's efforts. Take our positions and stand firm. Shine in the darkness. As a body of believers, we must stand united, fight against the works of darkness, and speak the name of Jesus. As He gives you a vision of a work to do, go forth by faith. In the Bible, there is an example of dry bones that hear the Word of the Lord and come alive as a vast army. In the Bible, there is an example of dry bones that hear the Word of the Lord and come alive as a vast army. This is a call to all of us who stand by faith in our Lord and Savior, Jesus Christ.

Ezekiel 37:1-14 says, *"The hand of the Lord was on me, and he brought me out by the Spirit of the Lord and set me in the middle of a valley; it was full of bones. He led me back and forth among them, and I saw a great many bones on the floor of the valley, bones that were very dry. He asked me, "Son of man, can these bones live?" I said, "Sovereign Lord, you alone know." Then he said to me, "Prophesy to these bones and say to them, 'Dry bones, hear the word of the Lord! 5 This is what the Sovereign Lord says to these bones: I will make breath enter you, and you will come to life. I will attach tendons to you and make flesh come upon you and cover you with skin; I will put breath in you, and you will come to life. Then you will know that I am the Lord." So I prophesied as I was commanded. And as I was prophesying, there was a noise, a rattling sound, and the bones came together, bone to bone. I looked, and tendons and flesh appeared on them and skin covered them, but there was no breath in them. Then he said to me, "Prophesy to the breath; prophesy, son of man, and say to it, 'This is what the Sovereign Lord says: Come, breath, from the four winds and breathe into these slain, that they may live." So I prophesied as he commanded me, and breath entered them; they came to life and stood up on their feet—a vast army. Then he said to me: "Son of man, these bones are the people of Israel. They say, 'Our bones are dried up and our hope is gone; we are cut off.' Therefore prophesy and say to them: 'This is what the Sovereign Lord says: My people, I am going to open your graves and bring you up from them; I will bring you back to the land of Israel. Then you, my people, will know that I am the Lord, when I open your graves and bring you up from them. I will put my Spirit in you and you will live, and I will settle you in your own land. Then you will know that I the Lord have spoken, and I have done it, declares the Lord."*

The Lord calls us from darkness to light, giving us the authority to shine in the darkness. These dry bones shall live. Hear the Word of the Lord spoken over you and alive in you. Let us take our positions and stand firm in Him. Time after time, disappointed, I refused to stand firm. Not that I had lost faith; I just felt that God had let me down. In these moments, I would speak doubtful words and fail to express my faith. I didn't understand favors. In my mind, favor meant God making a way for me. And that's true. However, I had to learn that the process of creating space for myself may require some repositioning.

This doesn't mean that God's favor is not on you. Although it may not seem like it, God's favor reveals itself at the appointed time. We must stand firm and trust His word. The vision God has given you has a purpose. It will surely come to pass. It will come against all hell, and it may seem impossible. Speak the truth and stand firm. Speak the truth and remain firm when a vast army forms against you and the situation appears hopeless. Take advantage of these situations. Let doubt and fear not overpower you. Use these opportunities to praise his name and stand firm. Guard your mouth and speak His truth. God is able to turn a situation around and make you a witness to His deliverance.

The kings dispatched messengers to Jehoshaphat, asserting that no one could resist them. People will try to convince you that it is hopeless. Take your position and stand firm. As these situations arise in your life, your faith in Him will grow. Understand the repositioning process. If what you are expecting God to do doesn't happen the way you thought, stand firm. He is working on it for your benefit. Grow in these truths and gain a deeper understanding of God's ways. His Word provides us with numerous examples of His Ways and Truths. These truths come to you through Jesus. Take your position and stand firm.

15

The Last Supper

Luke 22:7-8 says, *"Then came the day of Unleavened Bread on which the Passover lamb had to be sacrificed. Jesus sent Peter and John, saying, "Go and make preparations for us to eat the Passover."* The Day of Unleavened Bread is celebrated to remember the Israelites journey through the wilderness. This eleven day journey to the Promise Land was a forty year struggle. The number forty is depicted a lot throughout Scripture to symbolize a time of testing. Jesus fasted for forty days and forty nights and was tempted by the devil. Here the Israelites wandered in the wilderness for forty years.

I was thirty five years old when I truly cried out to Jesus. I still had a lot of growing to do over the next several years. I still have a lot of areas to grow in today. In my opinion it takes around forty years of life's experiences to come to the realization of needing a Savior. Some may disagree with that assessment. Its just my opinion. The forty years that the Israelites wandered in the wilderness has symbolic meaning to me. The mid life crisis of coming to know Jesus wholeheartedly. I know of people coming to know Jesus early in life who have lived a life of service for the Lord. I'm really speaking of the stubbornness and rebelliousness of myself.

Go and make Preparations, is what Jesus instructed Peter and John to do. Jesus gives us the way of Preparation. Just like He instructed Peter and John to do, we are to see the insight of His Instructions. In Luke chapter 21 Jesus is conversing with His Disciples concerning the end times and what is to come. There will be wars and rumors of wars. Earthquakes, famine, and pestilence in various places. There will be signs in the sun, moon and stars. Jesus ends His discussion of these end time events with a warning to all of us.

Luke 21:34-36 says, *"Be careful, or your hearts will be weighed down with carousing, drunkenness and the anxieties of life, and that day will close on you suddenly like a trap. For it will come on all those who live on the face of the whole earth. Be always on the watch, and pray that you may be able to escape all that is about to happen, and that you may be able to stand before the Son of Man."* The day of Unleavened Bread, the journey through the wilderness, depicts the anxieties of life. Be on guard and not give the enemy a foothold. Go and make Preparations. Jesus gave Peter and John instructions. In doing so He relays Spiritual Truths to us through His Instructions.

Luke 22:7-13 says, *"Then came the day of Unleavened Bread on which the Passover lamb had to be sacrificed. Jesus sent Peter and John, saying, "Go and make preparations for us to eat the Passover." "Where do you want us to prepare for it?" they asked. He replied, "As you enter the city, a man carrying a jar of water will meet you. Follow him to the house that he enters, and say to the owner of the house, 'The Teacher asks: Where is the guest room, where I may eat the Passover with my disciples?' He will show you a large room upstairs, all furnished. Make preparations there." They left and found things just as Jesus had told them. So they prepared the Passover."*

Following a man carrying a jar of water depicts being led by the Spirit of God. Its also a calling of the man carrying the jar of water as one who leads according to the Spirit of God. As they entered the house they were instructed to the guest room. Depicting the mind. Its in our minds, or Temple Courts, where guests or messengers come to visit. The large room upstairs is confirming where the guest room is located. Some of us have large heads so I find humor in the Wording. Its like Jesus said it so there's no mistaking what He's talking about. Its humorous to me. The large guest room is all furnished. Depicting having knowledge of the Word of God alive in you. It's the application and understanding of how to apply it.

So Jesus says make preparations there. Making the preparations is our ability to utilize what God has given us through His Word. The Passover is the celebration of the death Angel passing over the Israelites as they were held in slavery in Egypt. They were given strict instructions to follow that would symbolize their house being covered by the Blood of the Lamb. The death Angel passing over Egypt struck the houses not covered by the Blood of the Lamb and killed the first born son of each household. By following the Word of the Lord and obeying His Commands, the Israelites were passed over by the death Angel. This is the celebration of the Passover. It was this final plague that prompted Pharaoh to release the Israelites from slavery.

Jesus is the Lamb of God slain for our Redemption. Its His Blood applied to our lives that gives us life in Him. Its not by our works and by our hands that we have this Grace. Its through Faith in Him. Our Faith is expressed through following His instructions. Just like the instructions were given to the Israelites exactly what they should do in Preparation, we are given guidance from the Holy Spirit and the Word of God alive in us. Through Faith we have the Blood of Jesus applied to our lives.

Go and make preparations! As Jesus ate the Passover with His Disciples He invites each of us to eat with Him. Revelation 3:19-22 says, *"Those whom I love I rebuke and discipline. So be earnest and repent. Here I am! I stand at the door and knock. If anyone hears my voice and opens the door, I will come in and eat with that person, and they with me. To the one who is victorious, I will give the right to sit with me on my throne, just as I was victorious and sat down with my Father on his throne. Whoever has ears, let them hear what the Spirit says to the churches."* What an Honor it is to sit with Jesus and eat. The invitation to eat with Jesus still stands. He is knocking. That knocking sound can come through turbulent winds of life's circumstances, but He's still knocking. It took a pounding on the door for me to answer. But Glory be to God I finally opened up to Him. The process of my life changed. Its all about Jesus, His Sacrifice, and His Life in me. Opening the door to Jesus, I then had some growing to do. Throughout this process I had to learn Him and be in relationship with Him. Its about having my name written in Heaven. He knows me. He wants to have relationship with you too. Jesus instructed His Disciples when they were full of joy because the evil spirits submit to them in His Name.

Luke 10:17-20 says, *"The seventy-two returned with joy and said, "Lord, even the demons submit to us in your name." He replied, "I saw Satan fall like lightning from heaven. I have given you authority to trample on snakes and scorpions and to overcome all the power of the enemy; nothing will harm you. However, do not rejoice that the spirits submit to you, but rejoice that your names are written in heaven."* The entire process of Discipleship is Discipline. Learning to obey His Voice. Not that you are perfect in the sense of what we understand perfection. Being mature in understanding His Direction for our lives.

Trusting in Him as we grow in Him. The devil would love nothing more than to deceive you into thinking just because you believe you can live how you want to. Living this way is the act of denying Jesus before others. Jesus said if you deny Him, He will also deny you before the Father. Its a wake up call to Discipleship and the obedience that brings promotion and calling in your lives. Jesus gave the instructions to His Disciples to Go and make

Preparations. Notice as they obeyed their identity changed from Disciples to Apostles. Luke 22:14-16 says, *"When the hour came, Jesus and his apostles reclined at the table. And he said to them, "I have eagerly desired to eat this Passover with you before I suffer. For I tell you, I will not eat it again until it finds fulfillment in the kingdom of God."*

The Disciples didn't realize the Passover was also them passing over from Disciples to Apostles. When the hour came and Preparation was made. Their obedience as Disciples brought their purpose and identity to them. Did they make mistakes afterwards? Yes, Peter even denied Jesus. However, their destiny was established through their obedience and discipline. God used the denial of Jesus from Peter and made him a voice proclaiming Jesus going forward. The same is true for us. Standing firm in Him.

The fulfillment of the Kingdom of God is your complete obedience to Him. Jesus said I will not eat it again until it finds fulfillment in the Kingdom of God. A lot of people fail to understand the Kingdom of God. The Pharisees questioning Jesus asked about the coming Kingdom of God. Luke 17:20-21 says, *"Once, on being asked by the Pharisees when the kingdom of God would come, Jesus replied, "The coming of the kingdom of God is not something that can be observed, nor will people say, 'Here it is,' or 'There it is,' because the kingdom of God is in your midst."* Romans 14:17-18 says, *"For the kingdom of God is not a matter of eating and drinking, but of righteousness, peace and joy in the Holy Spirit, because anyone who serves Christ in this way is pleasing to God and receives human approval."*

The Last Supper before Jesus was crucified is the culmination of what everything in creation means. Past, present and future. Jesus was the Word of God Spoken from the beginning, also made flesh and dwelt among us, and is broken and given to us in Remembrance of Him as He lives in us. The drink is His Blood that is poured out for us and washes away our sin. All of the examples of Scripture in the Old Testament is for our learning of the Truth of Jesus alive in us. Whether we choose to believe that Truth by Faith or brush it off as unbelief is what each of us will have to give an account for on Judgment Day.

Jesus commissions the Disciples in Matthew instructing them to go and make Disciples. Matthew 28:18-20 says, *"Then Jesus came to them and said, "All authority in heaven and on earth has been given to me. Therefore go and make disciples of all nations, baptizing them in the name of the Father and of the Son and of the Holy Spirit, and teaching them to obey everything I have commanded you. And surely I am with you always, to the very end of the age."* The making of Disciples is the teaching of obedience to Jesus. The working of the Holy Spirit leads us into all Truth. If we cause those to stumble by becoming a stumbling block that leads them into error, woe is me! One plants, another waters, God gives the increase. The increase is given by being obedient to Him. Each of our lives is unique and complex in a variety of different ways. The calling of God will work what your experiences are and turn it into His Purpose. The Perfect Will of God for our lives.

God gave us the law to expose the sinfulness of sin. Jesus sends us His Spirit which works in accordance with all Truth. Exposing the sinfulness of sin then gives the Spirit grounds to guide our ways into Truth. We are given Grace through Faith in what Jesus done for us to shape our lives in accordance with His Will. The grace we are given is not a license to sin freely. The debt of sin has been paid through faith in Jesus. Now the work of Jesus in our lives is to shine out of darkness. Being partakers of His Divine Nature.

2 Peter 1:3-11 says, *"His divine power has given us everything we need for a godly life through our knowledge of him who called us by his own glory and*

goodness. Through these he has given us his very great and precious promises, so that through them you may participate in the divine nature, having escaped the corruption in the world caused by evil desires. For this very reason, make every effort to add to your faith goodness; and to goodness, knowledge; and to knowledge, self-control; and to self-control, perseverance; and to perseverance, godliness; and to godliness, mutual affection; and to mutual affection, love. For if you possess these qualities in increasing measure, they will keep you from being ineffective and unproductive in your knowledge of our Lord Jesus Christ. But whoever does not have them is nearsighted and blind, forgetting that they have been cleansed from their past sins. Therefore, my brothers and sisters, make every effort to confirm your calling and election. For if you do these things, you will never stumble, and you will receive a rich welcome into the eternal kingdom of our Lord and Savior Jesus Christ."

Having understanding of the significance of our works and the expression of our Faith is important. Building on the foundation which is Jesus Christ, our works will be tested and judged. 1 Corinthians 3:12-15 says, *"If anyone builds on this foundation using gold, silver, costly stones, wood, hay or straw, their work will be shown for what it is, because the Day will bring it to light. It will be revealed with fire, and the fire will test the quality of each person's work. If what has been built survives, the builder will receive a reward. If it is burned up, the builder will suffer loss but yet will be saved—even though only as one escaping through the flames."* As we ask the Lord to search our hearts and reveal to us what is not of Him, I pray that we listen and obey. If we humble ourselves before Him and confess our ways and repent He is Faithful and Just to forgive us and cleanse us from all unrighteousness. Let us seek vision as we meditate on His Words.

As He makes known to us His Words let us pray for Strength and guidance and discipline to carry out His Will for our lives. May He Sanctify us with His Truth, His Word is Truth. Let us take heed to the Holy Spirit which lives in us and obey His Guidance. 2 Chronicles 7:14 says, *"If My people who are called by My Name, will humble themselves and pray and seek My Face and turn from their wicked ways, then I will hear from Heaven, and I will forgive their sin and will heal their land."* The continuous act of humbling myself before God and confessing my faults has become a daily habit. Establishing my identity in Him and Speaking His Truth to my current circumstances enables my Hope to remain firm.

I am confident in the Lord and I know that His Word shall not fail. I am currently at the Red Eagle Work Center located in Montgomery Alabama. I am a Minister who regularly preaches the Word of God. I've transferred to different locations and no matter where I go I'm witnessing a movement of the Power of God taking place in prison. The experiences and encounters of the Spirit filled services are amazing. Watching the Lord work in peoples lives is truly a blessing. We are living in a time where the Outpouring of the Spirit is taking place. Let us unify in the Lord and Stand Firm together in Jesus Name. It's all about Jesus, thank You Lord!

About the Author

I was born on October 15, 1980, in Jasper, Alabama. I graduated from Parrish High School in 1999. Since being incarcerated in 2002 I went through a transformation from a drug-addicted and hopeless man to a purpose-driven man preaching the Word of God in prison. I am serving a life sentence in the Alabama Department of Corrections. More importantly, I am serving Life Eternally through Jesus Christ. I have completed numerous programs of rehabilitation and faith-based classes. I am a graduate of Transformational Ministry while incarcerated and currently a Minister in the facility.